T0365311

# Praise for *Beautiful Nate*

In *Beautiful Nate* author Dennis Mansfield is painfully, brutally honest—about the life and death of his son Nate; about grief and loss and failure; and still manages, convincingly, to point the reader to joy, hope, and fulfillment. It is about triumphing over grief and shedding crippling guilt. It is more than just a powerfully written book of remembrance and confession. *Beautiful Nate* is an affirmation of the faithfulness of Jesus. As He says in John 16:33, "In the world you will have trouble—heartache, tribulation, and loss—but take heart; I have overcome the world."

—Bodie and Brock Thoene, authors of *Icon*

Life is complex and at many times very painful—especially when the human heart is filled with unquenchable love for someone who never seems able to fully accept it. Although Dennis Mansfield's book *Beautiful Nate* tells the heartrending narrative of a parent's unrelenting love for one such boy, it does not deliver a message of despair, but rather one of authentic thanksgiving. This book conveys a gut-level honesty that Christianity in principle remains very nonreligious. It is an encouragement for all that we would not accept rejection based on the behavior of a person—but instead to love and give thanks for the glimpses God provides that illuminate the depth of who they truly are.

—Tri Robinson, author and founding pastor of Boise Vineyard Church

I've known Dennis for a long time and as a father I'm eager to read and learn what he has learned through such sorrow.

—John Eldredge, author of *Wild at Heart*

Have you ever sobbed deep in your soul? Throughout *Beautiful Nate*, Dennis Mansfield's very vulnerable faith journey, he teaches each of us this profoundly simple truth: soul-deep pain can be a great teacher forcing us to keep focused on our family and, even more important, on our Lord.

—Bobb Biehl, executive mentor, board of directors member of Focus on the Family, and author of numerous books

It is easy as parents to be self-righteous when *our* children make wise choices and do not rebel—or to labor under an almost unbearable sense of failure when our children do not make wise choices. *Beautiful Nate* knocks us off our self-righteous pedestal and lifts us up from our gutter of failure and helps us see God's desire and ability to meet us and love us in the midst of whatever our experiences are. Dennis tells his story with complete transparency, with a refreshing lack of platitudes, and laced with hope in a God who is able to bring life again to our dying souls and to redeem our most difficult experiences. *Beautiful Nate* is not a parenting book, but it will help you be a better parent. It is not a self-help book, but it will be helpful to you. It is not a theological treatise, but will help you wrestle with who God is. You will find yourself laughing at times, pondering often, and feeling tears as you live through life's most cruel twists with Dennis and Susan. You will also see how God is meeting them, and in the process I believe you will meet God as well.

—Drs. Paul and Virginia Friesen, founders of Home Improvement Ministries and directors of Family Camp at Campus by the Sea, Catalina Island, California

Dennis Mansfield tells a poignant, heartrending story of a Christian family where everything was supposed to turn out all right, but didn't. This is the true account of a beloved son's wayward choices and the devastating effects on his family. Dennis's honest, soul-searching narrative serves to challenge some of the unrealistic expectations and false promises of formula-driven performance Christianity. Some will find comfort and camaraderie in discovering they are not the only ones who've read the books and heard the sermons and tried their best to do it right, only to find that family life in this world under the curse is not as simple or predictable as believers sometimes pretend. Yet there remains a hopeful note throughout—there is a redemptive God whose story is not done.

—Randy Alcorn, author of *Heaven*

An experience with addiction hits close to home. Many want to talk about it but don't, many want to ignore it but can't, many want to fix it but don't know how. It's lonely, scary, and can drive a family apart—unless God comes into this equation. This book will make you cry, make you laugh, and educate you on the real life of addiction and the impact on a family and how God can heal what really seems permanently shattered. My friend, my brother in Christ, and his family tell their story!

—Pastor Tim D. Remington, Altar Church, Coeur d' Alene, Idaho, and director of Good Samaritan Rehabilitation

Nate was a beautiful young man, but like others his age, he made some mistakes. In our precious times together I was able to see Nate's heart and understand his confusion. I grieve Nate's untimely loss and believe the journey in this book will touch you—and bring hope to circumstances that are not often understandable.

—Melody Green, speaker, songwriter, cofounder of Last Days Ministries

The thing about life is that it is so daily! We never seem to know what to expect or what is around the corner. The one thing we can never anticipate, however, is the loss of a child. There is no manual or preparation for that. This book has a riveting message for everyone! I first met Nate when he was twelve and can still picture him dressed in a Boise State football uniform for Halloween. He was an eager, adventurous boy who loved life—he was a beautiful boy! His loss was huge; his parents and siblings were crushed and left with many tough questions and many memories. Nate's story, as told by his father, will captivate the reader and help change the lives of many as they read how this loving family is working its way through the most difficult challenge that any family can face—the loss of a child.

—Skip Hall, former Boise State head football coach

This story of two men, father and son, and their unfinished journeys, is a pearl bought at great price. It is a powerful book that looks at real life against the backdrop of a Christianity often painted in unrealistic colors. What happens when tragedy strikes a good Christian family? How to understand the loss of a son to drug abuse after following all the rules? This story of family conflict and human frailty nevertheless glows with the Lord's redemptive presence. I have had the honor of being Dennis's friend through much of this story, and I have been blessed to witness his pain, his struggles, and his faithfulness to Christ's love. Regardless of your deep loss or disappointment, this book will leave you with renewed hope in our Savior's relentless pursuit.

—David Ripley, political consultant, pollster, and founder of
Idaho Chooses Life

I am honored to call Dennis Mansfield a friend. He and his family have been through quite the journey, every step paved with many tears—every step paved with God's unyielding faithfulness. In this book, *Beautiful Nate*, Dennis takes you along with him on that journey, and there can be no doubt that your life will be richer for it. You will grow closer to your own family, discover new strength for your own life journey, and, more than anything, fall all the harder on God's most amazing grace.

—Bruce Marchiano, actor, author of *Jesus, the Man Who Loved Women* and *Jesus Wept*

It's a rare moment when a leader openly admits that he and his family are imperfect. *Beautiful Nate* provides us with one of these rare moments. With refreshing candor, Mansfield reveals the imperfection that is residing under his own roof. Transcending the "self-help" and "how-to" genres, *Beautiful Nate* is a vulnerable, courageous, real-life account of a family that is shaken to its core. From the tough-love scenarios of a family that actively allows one of their own to experience the consequences of his choices, to the unconditional love of a father who regularly visits his son in jail, Dennis Mansfield demonstrates that goodness—and love—can prevail through the worst of circumstances. For those of us who seek to better understand the "big things" in life, *Beautiful Nate* is required reading.

—Austin Hill, national talk show host and coauthor of *The Virtues of Capitalism*

*Beautiful Nate* captures the deep friendship and love of a father and son, as well as the subsequent difficulty involved in having that adult son be addicted to drugs. It also captures the hope that springs from being intentional as a family. The vulnerability and honesty of things that did not work is refreshing in Dennis Mansfield's work. There are no formulas in child raising. There is only the love of Christ, which then direct everything else. *Beautiful Nate* speaks candidly and openly about this truth.

—Gary and Norma Smalley, authors, Founders,
Smalley Relationship Center

# Beautiful
# Nate

*A Memoir of a Family's Love,
a Life Lost, and Heaven's Promises*

# Dennis Mansfield

HOWARD BOOKS
A DIVISION OF SIMON & SCHUSTER, INC.

*New York  Nashville  London  Toronto  Sydney  New Delhi*

Howard Books
A Division of Simon & Schuster, Inc.
1230 Avenue of the Americas
New York, NY 10020

First Howard Books hardcover edition March 2013

HOWARD BOOKS and colophon are trademarks of Simon & Schuster, Inc.

For information about special discounts for bulk purchases, please contact Simon & Schuster Special Sales at 1-866-506-1949 or business@simonandschuster.com.

The Simon & Schuster Speakers Bureau can bring authors to your live event. For more information or to book an event, contact the Simon & Schuster Speakers Bureau at 1-866-248-3049 or visit our website at www.simonspeakers.com.

Designed by Jaime Putorti

Manufactured in the United States of America

10  9  8  7  6  5  4  3  2  1

Library of Congress Cataloging-in-Publication Data

Mansfield, Dennis.
   Beautiful Nate : a memoir of a family's love, a life lost, and heaven's promises / Dennis Mansfield.
   p. cm.
   1. Mansfield, Nate, 1981–2009. 2. Children—Death—Biography.
3. Parenting. 4. Drug addiction. 5. Drug abuse. I. Title.

BF575.G7M345 2013
155.9'37085—dc23             2012023013

ISBN 978-1-4516-7861-1

*As an infant, Nate was dedicated to the Lord, a practice often employed by followers of Jesus. During that dedication, I gave up my firstborn son to the God who gave up his firstborn son for me.*

*This book is a type of second dedication:*
*to Nate, who awaits me in Heaven*
*to Meg, whom I love here on Earth*
*to Colin, who learned true life in Christ from his siblings*
*to my bride, Susan, the love of my life*

# Contents

Contents

## Part Three: In Loving Memory of Nate

*I am so very sad to hear of Nate's death, which is such a great tragedy and tremendous loss.*

*I am deeply saddened too.*

*I really liked Nate and saw so much potential and such a tender heart in him. But he was torn . . . in the valley of decision.*

*You are suffering more than words can possibly explain and I understand. It will take a while.*

*Nate's death will bring many to new life, although today that's probably not a great consolation . . . much better to have seen Nate come into a new life himself.*

*But in the years to come, it will be very meaningful for your family to see Nate's story change the stories of the lives of other young men and women.*

*Everyone has their own journey in these times but all can unify in the great loss of Nate the son, and Nate the brother.*

—Melody Green,
widow of recording artist Keith Green,
cofounder of Last Days Ministries

*Titus 2:11–14*
*The Message*

God's readiness to give and forgive is now public. Salvation's available for everyone! We're being shown how to turn our backs on a godless, indulgent life, and how to take on a God-filled, God-honoring life. This new life is starting right now, and is whetting our appetites for the glorious day when our great God and Savior, Jesus Christ, appears. He offered himself as a sacrifice to free us from a dark, rebellious life into this good, pure life, making us a people he can be proud of, energetic in goodness.

Nineteen eighty was a year of change. It brought about profound new worldviews and new directions that naturally flowed from them.

It was a time of strange cultural bedfellows. Ronald Reagan invited Americans to dream again and to do so without a dependence on government to help fulfill those dreams. As a presidential candidate, Reagan spoke openly about our need to protect the family unit, to pray together, and to help our neighbors.

John Lennon had settled down as a full-time dad to raise his son while his wife worked. Eventually, he began recording again. He released *Double Fantasy*, his first album in five years. On that album was the song "Beautiful Boy," dedicated to his youngest son, Sean.

Lennon sang of a world that included taking time for family and children, even taking time, as he wrote, to "say a little prayer" with your son or daughter.

The song mirrored Reagan's value of life and place of honor he said children should take in our lives. In part, Lennon's work on that final album reflected the dynamic tension in his life of living today while at the same time working for a future for his wife and son. He apparently even toyed with supporting Ronald Reagan for president in 1980, a recent documentary film contends (see http://jam.canoe.ca/Music/2011/06/28/18348856-wenn-story.html and http://beatlesstories.com/).

The lyrics and melody of John Lennon's song "Beautiful Boy" are his legacy to a childhood protected (see http://www.songmeanings .net/songs/view/8687/).

The chapters of this book take their cue from Lennon's work and often reflect Reagan's vision for family; they tell a story about a beautiful, beautiful boy named Nate. It is the journey of our first child and our subsequent trials about which I write.

Nate was born in 1981 and died in 2009.

But more than that, this book is about *your* life and letting you know that you're not alone in the current hard times for which you could never really have planned.

As John Lennon wrote in his song to his own son:

*Life is what happens to you,*
*While you're busy making other plans.*

# Part One

## Building the "Perfect" Family

# Chapter One

# Beautiful Nate

It was a pre-spring day like so many we'd experienced in lovely Boise, Idaho. The snow was melting, and green tulip bulbs were quietly sending leaf shoots on their way through the thawing earth. Like in so many other cold-weather states, sand or salt is often used as a slide inhibitor for the spots of sheer ice that you can see and the black ice that you cannot. As I walked from our home to my car in the driveway, I heard the soft *crunch, crunch, crunch* of sand underfoot. Once at work, walking from the parked car to the office, the same sound greeted my ears. It was just the normal sound of a normal close-of-winter day in our life. The calendar marked the day as March 11, 2009.

I'm a self-employed businessman; I almost always have been. In 2006, my business partner and I developed a new firm that housed ex-addicts and ex-inmates after they had completed their time in jail or prison. In the parlance of the industry, these houses are called "staffed, safe, and sober homes"; each normally has from five to twelve men or women. It's an unusual business and one that neither of us ever anticipated owning. Nonetheless, as businessmen, we saw a need to help ex-addicts, and we met that need with the tools and resources available to us. Both of us had sons who had brushes with the law due to drug abuse. Though our sons could not benefit personally from the houses that we developed (due to conflict of interest), as partners and fathers we saw how we could help other parents as they struggled with their sons and daughters in jail and in prison. Others joined us in putting time, treasure, and talent into this endeavor.

My wife, Susan, and I have three children: firstborn Nate; our second born, our daughter, Meg; and our caboose boy, Colin. We had an intentional, planned, and purposeful family. The kids grew up in a family environment of faith, fun, adventure, and travel. We often combined these elements and traveled across the globe, helping on foreign missions, assisting others who simply did not have the advantages we had as a family. Throughout these global jaunts, we would all be amazed at the commonality of people—regardless of the nation of region in which they lived. Children were born to parents, lived with them until maturity, and then went off to start their own lives. In the end, no matter what country, children became adults, parents passed away, and children buried their parents. This was the expected way to experience life.

On that date in March 2009, I left the office and went home to have lunch with my third child, Colin, then a homeschooled high school junior. Colin was attending a co-op school for home-educated kids, a school that brought students together twice a week in class and then allowed them to learn on their own for the other three days a week. On this day, my son was home working on math problems. Susan and our adult married daughter, Meg, were back at my office having their regular weekly Bible-study lunch with other women, including female ex-inmates. They came together once a week to mentor ex-addict women from a biblical perspective. Scripture was used as well as books from well-known female authors. The ex-inmates were treated with respect, honor, and dignity. Since the study was always held at lunchtime, food was provided, with special salads and hot dishes prepared by the non-addict women attendees. Laughter and joy were always present, as were frequent tears.

As I walked through the door of my house, my cell phone rang. It was Meg. "Dad, come back to the office immediately. We just got a call from Missouri. There's a problem with Nate." The silence behind the phone call was deafening. If there were sounds of women laughing or talking, I did not hear them. The call from my daughter was forcefully factual, straightforward, and crystal clear: "Come now."

There was a different tone in her voice than there had ever been during the previous ten years of dealing with her older brother's drug addiction. I hung up and turned to Colin. "Nate's in trouble again. Would you like to go with me to our office and find out what's going on?" My youngest son paused, thought about it, and nodded. We headed out our front door and heard the crunch of snow-mixed sand under our feet as we walked on the icy driveway to our family car.

We drove the two miles from our home to what was then our family's company office in complete and unusual silence, as if the Lord were preparing us for some very difficult times. As we got out of the car, we both looked slowly around the very normal outside comings and goings, similar to any office complex on any ordinary day, and then walked toward the entrance. Each step's crunch of sandy salt on the sidewalk seemed to carry with it a preamble of the gritty brokenness that awaited us.

As I opened the door, I heard the Lord quietly say to my spirit, *"Your life will never be the same once you open that door, but it will be all right."*

I walked in, turned the corner to my left, and saw my bride, Susan, sitting in a high-backed conference table chair next to our daughter and surrounded by their friends from the Bible-study lunch.

She was sobbing with tears I had never seen before. Susan looked up at me and said almost in a whisper, "Nate's gone. He's dead."

Emotions buckled my knees, and even as a man of faith, I fell sobbing and moaning against the back of a chair at that conference table. At twenty-seven years of age, our beautiful boy, Nate, was dead—apparently because of drugs.

*I was a leader in the national profamily movement. I loved my son. What happened to our intentional, planned, and purposeful parenting?*

My mind stopped. My heart nearly did as well.

How had our family come to this? I was a leader in the national profamily movement. I loved my son. What happened to our intentional, planned, and purposeful parenting?

All the family legislation and marriage conferences we worked on suddenly seemed to amount to nothing; all the homeschooling, all the summer vacation Bible schools, all our parental warnings of "the outside world," and all the energy in constructing a godly Christian barrier to that world seemingly amounted to nothing.

Why had all our efforts not worked?

# Chapter Two

# Finding Love,
# Then Finding the Lord

Susan and I fell in love during college. We each independently transferred to California Polytechnic University from our previous colleges not realizing that merely changing universities would completely change our lives. Susan's goal was to become an elementary school teacher, and I wanted to work in politics.

A chance meeting brought us together in a cute Southern California ice cream parlor where Susan waitressed during college. Susan later told me that as she approached the table where I sat, she heard herself ask the question: *I wonder if I'm going to marry that man?* But she quickly dismissed it as a silly thought. I had never met her before; we'd never talked with each other. Though I was seated at a table with a longtime girlfriend, as well as a close friend, Susan's sweet smile and caring demeanor immediately impressed me. There was something spiritual about her that appealed to me instantly as she approached the table, "Hello, my name is Susan, how may I serve you?"

That first visit to the restaurant was followed by others (only *without* my former companions). A first date was followed by other dates—all centered on the deeper things of life. Susan and I talked about God from the start of our friendship. Though neither of us were professed Christians, we were in no way antagonistic to the claims of Christ. That openness helped us as we searched for God.

Susan and I met in January 1977 during semester break and quickly fell in love. I proposed marriage on the Fourth of July, and we were married in November—all in that same year.

Shortly after we married we realized that there had to be more to a great marriage than just the two of us. Maybe we needed to add God to our life together. Both of us had been raised with an understanding of God, yet our knowledge seldom made its way into our daily lives. I was raised a Roman Catholic, and Susan was a nominal Episcopalian. We understood that a sense of religion was useful, yet we struggled with how something like faith could be of practical daily value. Even though no one showed us how to search for God, we decided to strike out and try to find Him on our own.

*Even though no one showed us how to search for God, we decided to strike out and try to find Him on our own.*

Not that God was missing from our lives entirely, mind you. It just seemed that whatever methods we were using to bring God into our early relationship somehow needed to be expanded.

After getting married in November, we celebrated our first Christmas together. We wanted Jesus in our lives, but we were a bit unsure how a little ceramic baby in a bundle of red and green cloths, surrounded by oxen, sheep, and oddball human characters could be of any real spiritual value to us. Yet we were open to it.

## Growing Up in the Sixties

Not unlike many young people in the 1960s and early '70s, Susan and I were eyewitnesses to the many cultural trends that had so impacted America. Kids who became teens in the 1960s saw division and assassinations, political hope and military loss. My adolescence was bookmarked first by John Kennedy's inaugural address of hope and vision, then later by Robert Kennedy's assassination and the buildup of our military presence in Southeast Asia, with president-elect Richard Nixon's unofficial campaign slogan being the ultimate cultural irony: "Bring us together."

In a way, though, I had an extra-special seat as an eyewitness to many of these events due to my family. As the son of a noncommissioned officer in the U.S. Air Force, my first childhood memory was of sitting on my father's shoulders watching President Dwight Eisenhower in his presidential limousine as he drove to the Capitol for his second inauguration, in January 1957. A few years later, while stationed in San Antonio, Texas, my father took my siblings and me to hear what would be President John F. Kennedy's last formal speech—the day before he was assassinated. Continuing to grow up in Texas, I regularly saw President Johnson's family, his cabinet members, and many heads of state who visited him there; all this between the ages of five and ten. When I was seventeen, President Nixon appointed me to the U.S. Military Academy at West Point. After he left office, five years later, we corresponded regularly until his death. My front-row seat as an eyewitness to the history of the 1960s and '70s allowed me, from my youth, to have a different perspective on important people and historical events.

The 1970s also gave full bloom to a different sort of historical icon; during the Jesus Movement, thousands of teenage Southern

Californians began searching for, and finding, deep and personal relationships with Jesus Christ.

Though eyewitnesses to the movement, Susan and I were not participants, at least not as it started. We were, however, interested observers. National news organizations like *Time* and *Newsweek* carried cover stories of young adults being born again. With the limited breadth of my religious awareness, I simply did not understand why a person would want to be born differently than he or she was originally born. It did not make sense to me and seemed like some sort of easy escapism. My father had taught me that when times were tough, you did not escape, you simply got tougher.

## Searching for Jesus

In our ignorance, Susan and I wandered through the great labyrinth of living by feelings. Both of us needed help in solving the puzzle of which specific religion was best for us. Susan knew a small number of born-again Christians, yet neither of us had the sense that we would ever embrace such a belief system.

Having left both our Catholic and Protestant roots, however shallow they were, Susan and I were hungry for something, *anything* that would feed our spirits. Many things offered to fill our void; however, not all of them are good, we discovered.

Some felt good—like Religious Science. We were married by a new-age Religious Science reverend, and our vows (as best we can now recall them) involved something about "staying together while everything is good" and "depending on father god/mother god" to help us maintain marital harmony as the years came at us.

The whimsically religious words seemed spiritual enough for me. I loved the service because I loved my bride.

Now, with a spiritual addition to our mix, I felt that I was on the edge of truly getting it—of knowing it all. Life seemed beautiful, religion seemed workable, and since Susan and I believed that we were all born good, I thought it simply couldn't get much better than this.

When a denomination offers its celebrants positive messages, absent the shadow of sin and Hell, there is a natural happiness that accompanies the services, rather than a supernatural joy. Many denominations that shy away from the traditional orthodoxy of the Christian faith feel that maintaining happiness and comfort for their supporters is the best route to take. Susan and I felt loved and welcomed in this environment. We simply did not know that we needed to be saved from sin and Hell.

But completing college as a young married couple took its toll. Work did, too. Stress began to build. Competing self-interests raised their ugly heads. There were more than a few angry shouting matches and slammed doors. Our apartment neighbors put up with so much from this terribly selfish set of newlyweds. *What have I done?* I asked myself. *Did I marry the wrong person?* I'm not sure Susan ever thought about divorce, but I believe any court would have given her mercy had she considered homicide. I was a self-centered jerk.

In desperation, we determined to begin attending the church service of the new-age pastor who married us. We needed another dose or two of happiness and good feelings that we knew his church service would

*Competing self-interests raised their ugly heads. There were more than a few angry shouting matches and slammed doors.*

provide. Most of the church services concluded with the same song's opening lyric: "Let there be peace on earth and let it begin with me." It always seemed to lighten the load of anger. Until the next conflict exploded.

Then in our first married spring, we decided to take in that same reverend's Easter service message. He began with these words: "Now, I don't want to sound like a Jesus freak today, but it's Easter and bear with me because I'd like to chat with you about him." Susan and I looked at each other surprised, as if to ask, *Isn't Easter the one time of the year that we* should *hear about Jesus? Why would that be considered a "freak" thing to do?* Since he didn't talk of the devil or of Hell, his message was funny and clever and even had a splash of hope. And despite his clearly disdainful review of blood and the Cross, his delivery was impeccable. He resembled Jimmy Carter in appearance and had that same sense of cardigan warmth about himself. But the death of Jesus was clearly an awkward thing for him.

After the service, Susan and I visited the church's bookstore and could not find any books about Jesus or the early church or the tenets of Christianity. We were disturbed. It left us with questions: What did these people believe? How could they not believe in Jesus? It honestly gave us the creeps, and we felt conflicted. On the one hand, we loved the pastor who married us and we loved attending the positive church services. We loved singing songs and hymns and we loved the messages of hope and future vision. Yet there was a sliver in our minds, and we were in pain and troubled at receiving what was clearly only half of Jesus' message. His death on the Cross meant something, yet it seemed so trivial to believe that the Son of God died on the Cross simply to make us happy.

Having determined that we'd eventually include children, by

birth or adoption, in our marriage, the necessity of finding a "good" church seemed a necessity. The idea that kids need to go to church somehow attached itself to us. First, it seemed, we ought to become well versed in that elusive thing called religion so that we could eventually lead any little ones on that same path. If religion didn't help us, even positive religion, we wondered what spiritual things would. We had no idea what to do.

And such a search would have to take place as we also sought our professional directions. At twenty-three years old, neither Susan nor I felt there was a rush to solve this spiritual problem, since we did not yet have any children on the way. It would be solved, we both felt, but we'd do it in our time, as we moved ahead with our careers.

Like so many other young couples with newly earned college degrees in the late '70s and early '80s, the doors for professional jobs in our chosen fields opened quickly for us. Employers needed solid employees. With President Reagan's election came economic good times. Susan was hired as a public school elementary teacher, and I was hired to help candidates in the Los Angeles GOP primary and general elections. During this time, I came in contact with the well-known political figures of that era: Reagan, Ford, Dole, Kemp, George H. W. Bush, and many others, including the founders of California's Proposition 13, Howard Jarvis and Paul Gann. My career in politics seemed to take off.

*If religion didn't help us, even positive religion, we wondered what spiritual things would. We had no idea what to do.*

We managed to keep ourselves busy so that the bickering would remain limited—but it *was* there. By our first wedding anniversary, an unintended Band-Aid for our afflictions came in the form of a puppy. This new acquisition necessitated a move at the pointed suggestion of an unhappy apartment manager. So we moved.

God's providence throughout these many quick events was amazing. The four words "hopeful," "hurt," "help," and "intentional" were with us all the time. We were a *hopeful* young couple who loved each other and also wanted to love God—yet we *hurt* each other and had no real *help*. We were *intentional* in our search for the Lord and equally *intentional* in our love for each other. We were young people, driven to actively pursue an elusive God. We would not give up.


## *Young Faith*

The Lord of the Universe did not give up on us, either; he did not let us down. He found us a house-behind-a-house to rent (for our puppy and for our souls). Our home's lawn was huge for the dog. The landlords' hearts were huge for us—they loved us and they loved our dog. Their house was directly in front of our little bunga-low. They were solid Christians.

Each Friday the landlords opened their home for a Bible study—something we had never attended. Eventually, we decided to join them. What we found was quite amazing. In the past, I would often mock people who were smokers or had the ugly tat-toos of the 1950s. It was also not beyond me even to mock those who participated in self-help groups like Alcoholics Anonymous. "I'm Tony and I'm a down-and-out-alcoholic, blah, blah," I would laughingly say to others.

The Bible study turned out to be an AA Bible study where

everyone smoked cigarettes. And under the blue haze of tobacco smoke hung the tattooed arms of searching men and women who held tightly to their Bibles. Initially, I did not want to be around these smelly, tattooed crybabies—they were not professional and they were not my type. But somehow my mockery no longer worked.

The Bible studies concentrated on the essentials of traditional Christian faith. I learned that man was created in God's image, that there *really* were two people named Adam and Eve, that their actions changed all of creation, and that mankind fell. I learned that Christ redeemed us and that Satan is real and that he'll spend eternity in Hell. I also learned that those who refuse to accept Jesus as their Savior and Lord would join him there. More important, these raw and unvarnished Friday-night Bible studies spoke of hope: I learned that Christ actually died for me and that this positive message was the clarion call for all mankind, for all who were willing to humble themselves before Him.

*Initially, I did not want to be around these smelly, tattooed crybabies—they were not professional and they were not my type.*

In the past, I did not want to hear of Hell and sin, but this small Bible-study group of ex-addicts and ex-inmates spoke truth with an eloquence far greater than anything I had ever heard from the reverend who married us.

In a wonderful twist of irony, God used the things I did not like to produce the things that saved my life and the life of my bride.

God brought all these people into our lives to lead us and show us a personal relationship with Christ. On January 20, 1980, Susan and I were baptized in the Christian faith. It seemed clear from the start that, as believers in Jesus, we needed only to pursue Him with our whole heart, soul, spirit, and mind and He would be there to solve our every need—almost like following a formula.

We lived from one miracle to the next. If we needed funds to pay rent because the paychecks were too short one month, we'd pray and then find an envelope of cash under our front doormat. When groceries were a bit light, God moved our friends, the VanderWendes, to buy a month's worth of food for us. We told no one of our plight, we simply prayed, observed, and marveled—time after time. Cars were fixed, lawn mowers worked, people showed up at the right time with the right solutions— no matter what the problems were. Christianity was real and *it worked!*

The words of the Bible sprang off the pages and burrowed deeply into our lives. I read for the first time that there were two feedings by Jesus of the thousands of people who followed him. I read of where the term "born-again" came from in the New Testament. In fact, I was blown away when I realized that it was Jesus who said, "You must be born again." I remember calling up a friend and saying, "Did you know that Jesus lived on Earth almost a month and a half *after* he rose from the dead?" My friend, a longtime Christian, must have smiled at the other end of the phone before he answered. I'll never forget what he said: "Wow, Dennis, that's awesome to hear. Tell me more." And I did.

I realized that the words of Jesus had life in them and nobody had ever really shared them with me—or if they did, I had failed to listen. Now I was all ears! I was not about to make that mistake with anyone else. I shared the good news of Jesus with everyone I met. I wore a small tie tack shaped like a fish, indicating an allegiance with Christ, to identify myself for other believers. I'll never forget during one lunch job interview I went on, I was asked what the most important thing in my life was. "It's my personal faith in Jesus Christ," I told the interviewer, "but don't worry, I don't wear it on my sleeve." The witty interviewer quickly grasped the moment: "No, I see that instead you wear it on your tie." I was sold out to the Lord and I didn't care who knew. Oh, by the way, I didn't get that particular job.

Susan and I listened to several Jesus Movement recording artists but really liked the music of an artist named Keith Green and his wife, Melody. Like an Old Testament prophet, Keith Green preached and sang hard about the hypocrisy of the Christian church in America. He was brutal in his condemnation of the liars and cheats who sold the Christian faith. In fact, after his music began to flourish and he was accepted by millions of listeners, he renegotiated his record company contract and made it possible for anyone at anytime to receive one or more of his albums, free of cost. He allowed them to donate, if they wished, so he could mail out more albums for free. He asked those who had substance to give more money so that those who had nothing could own his music, too. He read in the Bible that he was supposed to help those who were most needy, so he and his wife opened their own home to drug addicts and prostitutes who wanted to get out of their damaged lifestyles. He and Melody bought other properties for more houses to help more people. They gave away clothes and cars. Keith Green was radical in his faith. It was that exact radical level of Christianity that I wanted in my life—or at least I *thought* I wanted for Susan and me.

One Sunday we lay in bed skipping church because we were tired. But we were not too tired

*It was that exact radical level of Christianity that I wanted in my life—or at least I thought I wanted for Susan and me.*

to listen to Christian music. Keith Green's voice came from the record player:

> *How can you be so dead, when you've been so well fed,*
> *Jesus rose from the grave . . . and YOU . . . you can't even get out*
>   *of bed.*

We got up. We also grew up.

We never again intentionally missed assembling together with other believers. We realized how prone we are to roam and wander, so we made church attendance a concrete part of our lives. We were easily distracted by the world, and we found that one day a week in church helped us regain our bearing for the next week.

We realized that if we wanted to serve Jesus with our full hearts and minds, our legs and arms also needed to be a part of the Gospel. Keith Green's example of serving the Lord at full speed appealed to us. We wanted to start a legacy; we wanted to see our family aggressively serve the Lord.

If God would give us any children, we would raise them in the "nurture and the admonition of the Lord." Susan and I knew that having children would simply mean finding out what the Bible has to say about little ones, then following it word for word. Intentional parenting was our plan from the start.

Our unflinching loyalty to God and to His Word allowed us a freedom of purpose that was laced up tightly with books by then-fledging authors like Jim Dobson, Gary Bauer, and others; even Jimmy Carter spoke of being born-again. We read what they all had to say. Since we didn't have an evangelical Christian heritage, we determined to lean on the professionals who had gone before us. We came to believe that those who had public voices had much to tell us.

Almost every voice that met us from the car radio via Christian stations fed Susan and me as if every speaker knew exactly what we needed to grow. It was the most amazing and near magical of times.

## Intentional Parenting Begins

By the fall of 1980 we were pregnant with our first child. Susan and I attended Lamaze classes, learning all that we could about the intricacies of birthing children without using pain meds, allowing us the most natural childbirth experience possible. We knew what it meant to be intentional in our study of God's Word, and now it seemed we would know exactly what it meant to be intentional about childbirth and the subsequent child rearing. Though we had no help from our own folks regarding how to raise our soon-to-arrive baby (and we weren't quite sure we even *wanted* their advice), we determined to educate ourselves and become parenting experts. We would have it no other way; we would know *precisely* what to expect. We'd invite the baby into our world without changing a thing about our lives. That was what we thought purposeful, intentional Christians did. Little did we know that intentional parenting is much more than just inviting a helpless baby into a family circle as a passive participant. Rather, intentional parenting involves choosing each day to integrate children into the very culture of a family. It is not an event; it is a journey.

In one sense, my confidence in Christ verged on arrogance. We began to feel (and probably act) as though we knew it all. Or at least we believed we had learned what it took to be great parents. I even remember, after our first son was born, correcting my older brother, Gary, and sister-in-law, Jane, about how they were raising their three-year-old son, Kevin; giving unsolicited advice to him and feeling good about how much I knew, as the father of a three-month-old.

As a young man of new faith, I was about to begin my journey not only with my new Father but also with my new son.

I had no clue how little I actually knew and how much difficulty was about to come at my wife and me. Both of these realities were about to hit me squarely in the face.

# Chapter Three

# The Arrival of Children
# and Child-Centered Parenting

*In December 1980, John Lennon was shot to death on the front steps of the Dakota apartment building in New York City. His last words were reported to be "I'm shot," as he stumbled into the apartment's complex entrance.*

*In March 1981, President Reagan was seriously wounded in a very similar close-range assassination attempt in Washington, D.C. Upon surviving, Ronald Reagan privately wrote that he would dedicate the remaining years of his life "to serving Him."*

*Into that world of politics, music, and faith was born our son, Nathan Dennis Mansfield.*

Nate was born in Southern California in July 1981. Like so many evangelical parents in the early 1980s, we treated the birth of our children as if each were almost a holy event—for in comparison to how abortion had robbed so many couples of their children, it seemed to us to be a holy event. We saw God's face in the tiny little images of brand-new babies. Though we knew the admonition to worship only the Lord (and we felt we followed that admonition), there was a type of worship that accompanied the birth of many babies within the Christian community of thirty years ago. In many ways, the Christian community has always appreciated and embraced newborn children, since Scripture speaks repeatedly of the importance of raising children. The most noteworthy verse states that they should be raised so that when they grow up "they will not depart" from the Lord. But something seemed different in the years of the Jesus Movement and beyond.

Child-centeredness is a behavioral pattern that, among many other things, allows the child to gain center stage in the family, with the parents treating the infant, toddler, elementary school child, and then young adult primarily as a friend. The child sets the tone and direction for the family, rather than the parents. Child-centeredness became the Christian community's response to the secular world's discarding of infants in the womb by abortion.

## Every Child a Worshipped Child

On the one hand, Planned Parenthood assisted in the deaths of millions of babies in utero, so that the parents would be free of child-raising responsibilities. Planned Parenthood's initial motto was "Every child a wanted child," but within the Christian community, on the other hand, an equally offensive motto took hold: "Every child a worshipped child." Child-centeredness set the stage for a different type of child rearing than had ever been done before. The personal worth and value of the child were clearly acknowledged, yet without proper discipline boundaries, it set the stage for a fear-based selfishness that arose in the parents and, ultimately, in the children being raised.

Intentional parenting anchors itself to timeless, proven truths for all children. Child-centeredness treats an individual child as if he or she is so unique that no general rules of behavior apply to him or her. Intentional parenting encourages a selflessness that trumps the selfishness of child-centeredness. Children take their cues from whichever approach their parents choose.

At what point do intentional parenting and child-centeredness cross? That was what we were about to find out.

After I greeted the newborn baby Nate and saw that the mother and baby were fine, I left the hospital and fell exhausted into my mini-truck. As I turned the ignition key, the radio automatically came on, and the opening lines of Harry Chapin's haunting song "Cat's in the Cradle" met me.

I shook with awe and surprise at the timing of this song. And I also wept with fear.

*At what point do intentional parenting and child-centeredness cross? That was what we were about to find out.*

I wept for what I feared might happen in Nate's life and in our lives together. My own life with my father was captured in the tortured lyrics of that song. My dad, Bill Mansfield, was a good man who had a mean and angry mother and a life that poisoned him on many levels. His mother did not treat him with honor, and he inadvertently carried on that tradition with his seven children. He sought solace in his professional career—both as a noncommissioned officer between the 1940s and 1960s and as a pioneer in the start-up computer industry of the mid-1960s. Dad worked hard and seldom saw us. What he never got from his parents, he never gave to us: intimacy and time.

I did not want the "Cat's in the Cradle" lyrics to represent my future relationship with my son. In a determined desire to avoid the pain of the past, I sought an intentional and purposeful path for the future—on the very day my first child was born. I would be a *much* better father to my son than my own dad had been to me. Without knowing it, child-centeredness became a key part of my life at that very point. In tears, I drove the four or so miles to our house, sobbing as the song continued.

It was there and then that I dedicated myself to live as an intentional father for Nate (and any other kids that could, and did, come along)—to not be swept away by my career and the foolish things that tend to occupy our precious minutes on this Earth. Right from the start, child-centeredness, however quiet and deceitful, intertwined itself with my intentionality, without me even knowing it.

## The Weed Seeds of Child-Centered Parenting

Looking to the future, I vowed that the words of that song would definitely not apply to Nate's life or mine, should we both be blessed to advance in age. Intentional parenting would mean that I would strive to parent with a purpose, studying the leaders of the day, finding out what it would take to produce a child who loved God and served Him all of his days.

*Our goal of intentional parenting was immediately tainted with the weed seeds of child-centered parenting.*

But what I did not realize was that the seed of child-centered parenting had been planted in my heart and would play a significant role in how we parented our children—especially Nate. Our goal of intentional parenting was immediately tainted with the weed seeds of child-centered parenting.

## *The Plant Shoots of Intentional Parenting*

Just as weed seeds can accidentally be scattered by child-centeredness, intentional parenting allows for a clear planting of newly budded shoots that are placed in the soil with creative freedom and purposeful intent: strategic ends accomplished, at times, by vague and spontaneous tactical actions. The goals are in concrete; the plans are in sand.

For example, Susan and I put a premium on planned moments of fun. Varying bedtime stories were told every night, hide-and-go-seek happened inside our home with the lights out at the drop of a hat, soccer coaching involved playing tag on the practice field rather than practicing soccer, mission trips were taken to

*The goals are in concrete; the plans are in sand.*

interesting places on other continents. Our family saved every cent we had and traveled to the Olympics in Atlanta; we took annual vacations in our car, creating a love for road trips by all of us. The kids did service projects, and I took them to work with me. My kids and I took walks around the neighborhood, creating adventures and fighting invisible foes on our way to get candy. We always had family pets, even snakes and gerbils. Our holiday traditions included placing straw in Baby Jesus' manger, awaiting Christmas morning, when the precious ceramic Savior would arrive. Our family had special meals, we ate off of birthday plates, held special birthday parties—our friends called our celebrations national holidays because they meant so much to all of us (and we all took the day off!). We talked politics so that our children would be informed. I ran for office and included the kids in the campaigns. We parented with intentionality.

Near the end of Nate's life, during our last road trip together, he and I were alone as we drove through the night, and we discussed the song "Cat's in the Cradle." He and I came to the conclusion that Harry Chapin's words had not defined our lives together as father and son. His story lyrics were not the words to our story, and we both rejoiced. Intentional parenting allowed us to be together. At odds with such intentional parenting, though, was Nate's drug use, which seemed to spring out of our child-centered approach.

As my father had unintentionally copied his mother's method of child rearing and therefore produced very unsavory fruit in his own child raising, I was purposeful in not following my historical lineage and, therefore, doing other positive and intended things that would produce fruit in the lives of my children.

How strange it is that the criticisms, negative actions, and default reactions of an unintentional generation can cause deep personal wounds, as in the case of my father's upbringing. Yet, in an intentional generation, as in the case of my son's upbringing, there remains no guarantee of the outcome either. Nate made a clear decision that he wanted to find out about the ugly side of life, because he was Nate-centered.

As we strove to parent with wise, thoughtful intentionality, the tentacles of child-centered parenting intertwined themselves with our best intentions—and the results would be devastating.

Intentionality, though key to raising a solid family, cannot alone be the defining element for success. It takes, among other things, a deep love to overcome the anger brought about by children's self-centered, bad behavioral choices.

## Welcome Insights

On that same trip, near the end of Nate's life, he spoke of how much he appreciated growing up in our family and being loved by my wife and me. Nate spoke of the fun he had living in an adventurous home—one that was a little bit crazy and had a whole lot of love. He reminisced about the way his mother and I purposely focused on each of our kids and how that helped him grow as a confident person. He soberly told me, though, that his choices with drugs were purely his choices and did not reflect how he was raised. He wanted to take drugs for his own self. He chose to do drugs. It was that simple.

Hearing him tell me that, as his parents, we had done so many things well was a blessing. That he had not followed our admonition to stay away from drug use was insanity to me. It was like hearing a departing spouse say how great the marriage was, only to end it by saying, "and because of that, I have decided to divorce you."

My wife and I came to understand that Nate chose to take drugs out of his own personal curiosity and rebellion. He felt good while taking those drugs. What he failed to understand was that eventually those drugs would take him. The insanity and chaos created by Nate's abusing illegal and prescription drugs brought my wife and me into a totally different universe. We were deeply conflicted between the worlds of intentional and child-centered parenting.

The change between little boy Nate and his adult version was almost too huge to comprehend. The years of his childhood had clarity and order to them. His teen years had only chaos, with slight, thin breaches of sanity, allowing us to peer in and see the Nate who really was.

## Meg's Arrival

Meg arrived in 1984—three years and two months after Nate's birth. When she was born, she had the umbilical cord wrapped many times around her neck, and the too-young doctor seemed scared and unsure as he unwound the cord from the brand-new baby girl's neck—almost like a frightened fisherman with a tangled line. I remember thinking to myself, *This is not a big deal; we prayed for a safe delivery and God always gives us exactly what we pray for.* I lived in the secure confidence (shall I say arrogance) that Jesus gives parents the very things they ask him for. Even considering the death of a newborn was impossible for me. *Nope,* I said to myself; *my Jesus always delivers live babies.*

Megan lived, as I knew she would. Formulas of faith give a strange kind of false confidence in any and every situation. Youthful parenting has a certain level of foolish bravado to it. As a young man, I was certainly a participant.

No Harry Chapin songs met me in my vehicle after I tucked in mother and baby daughter for their hospital stay. It was strangely similar in other ways to Nate's birth, with the same hospital and possibly even the same floor and delivery room— but absolutely different, for I now had a son *and* a daughter.

I felt I was an expert at being a father of a son, but the idea of conquering a new learning curve for a daughter initially seemed a bit unnerving to me. But I remember thinking in the hospital's parking lot as I climbed once again into our blue mini-truck for my drive home, *Well, I became an expert rather quickly with my little boy; I'm sure I can do the same with a little girl.* Arrogance, it seems, has its own sense of perception.

*Arrogance, it seems, has its own sense of perception.*

## Expert Status Meltdown

Years ensued, and sibling rivalry began to show me just how much I did *not* know about rearing the different sexes. I often felt like a policeman in the middle of a gang fight. No kidding! I could not, for the life of me, understand how two children raised by such experts could end up looking and sounding as though they were auditioning for roles in *Lord of the Files.* Petty jealousy and anger between them often blunted what were intended to be happy moments. I can remember being utterly embarrassed at my children's behavior—at church, with family, in public. It was excruciating. Our unintentional child-centered parenting was not working.

Susan and I both grew up in large families, so a family with only two opposite-sex children was new to us. We often tried to have the kids play with each other, but it seemed always to end up as a fistfight or a yell fest. Each child would rat out the other one the minute he or she caught the opponent in some perceived wrongdoing. Susan and I bought books on sibling rivalry, listened to radio programs from Focus on the Family, went to seminars about child rearing, and asked for help from friends and family.

It was exhausting!

Still, attempting to regain our supposed expert status, we bought and followed the books from the Christian bookstores, and eventually we seemed to get the rowboat righted and all the oars going in the same direction. Useful on more than a few occasions to our young family were some of the works of Dr. James Dobson and Focus on the Family. We often listened to his radio program and found it helpful through some of the land mines of parenting. In particular, I remember hearing Dr. Dobson speak about the "first adolescence" and how toddlers found their way to that level of independence, creating anger and misunderstanding in many families. It turned out we were just such a family.

The first adolescence of our children was tougher than anything we had faced so far, but we pressed on. Our toddlers were angry and so self-absorbed that I remember thinking to myself, *If this is the* first *adolescence, how in the world are we going to make it through their second adolescence, when they really* are *teenagers?* Time would indeed be our teacher, as we mulled over that question.

It seemed never ending. I remember saying to Susan, "Where did those two experts go who used to take care of our infants?" Hesitant laughter would follow, but the irony of my rhetorical question was not lost on either of us. We found out later that many of those sibling slugfests, though normal in many families, created a division between our two oldest children that would follow them into adulthood.

And time moved forward.

## *Intentional and Child-Centered Parenting Intertwined*

Every birthday was a celebration; I took off from my self-employed work, so that the birthday boy (or girl) would enjoy our time together. We would be making intentional memories, I reasoned. In one sense, we took time off to show our kids that we loved them. In another sense, we took time off for ourselves. Being intentional as parents carried a cost. Susan and I chose time with our family rather than with friends. I remember choosing not to pursue certain employment opportunities because they would take me away from my family. Our intentional efforts became weighted on the side of child-centered parenting.

Susan and I felt that even if our expert-parent badges were a bit bent, twisted, and splattered by spaghetti sauce, we believed that our intentional parenting still shined and would eventually win our children's hearts. Little did we know that our efforts were more child-centered than anything else. Each day we'd get up, plant our feet, and face new "challenges" (as the positive child-rearing books asked us to call them). And we did. We thought we were being intentional about their childhood. When conflict occurred I often would guilt my kids by asking how they could act in such a bratty fashion when we had poured out such moments of fun and recreation. In essence, I refused to allow our children to own their feelings. Rather than being intentional—or even child-centered—I was sometimes self-centered. My selfishness stood as a glaring example for them to imitate.

## Colin Joins the Family

Rounding out our trio of children is Colin. We had the advantage of having a seven-year spread between his sister and him, with a decade-plus dividing him and his brother, Nate.

The much-anticipated birth of a third child really can become a family affair. Siblings see their mom's advance through the clear and obvious stages of pregnancy, reacting and responding to each new development. Our family was no different. Nate and Meg loved seeing the physical changes happen with their mom, each placing bets with the other on the possible date of birth, the sex, and the name. The intimacy of having a third child coming late in all of our lives allowed the two older kids to anticipate the birth positively and embrace each other as well as their new sibling, once the birth date arrived.

And that date happened in April, yet with a terrible twist.

Susan and I opted to give birth to our new baby in a French-style water-birthing system. Placed in a bathtub, the mom is able to share in seeing the baby birthed beneath the waterline, thereby allowing those present to almost have a view of how the baby existed in the womb, before the infant breaks the waterline and begins breathing. All that we read about the then new birthing technique helped increase the anticipation of the child's birth. We were fully prepared for this amazing opportunity.

But what happened the day of delivery is seared into my memory as if it happened yesterday. A baby boy arrived. He was under the waterline of the expansive tub, as planned—yet only for an instant.

The attending physician thrust his hands down into the tub, immediately severing the umbilical cord—all in one motion.

The tiny infant was whisked to a medical tabletop, just out of Susan's and my view. The doctor worked ferociously on the little one. I could see from the corner where I was seated with Susan, as she fell back on my legs in the tub, that something was terribly wrong. We strained to see what was happening and waited as our doctor attempted several forms of resuscitation on this new little child. Minutes ticked away: five, seven, eleven. It was unbearable. My wife asked the only question I can remember from that eternity of unending minutes: "The baby's dead, isn't it?"

I decided to act; exiting the birthing tub and drying myself off at the legs, I walked quickly over to the doctor. I stood next to him and prayed. Fourteen minutes went by, then sixteen. I placed my arm on the doctor's shoulder and looked down on the fully extended body of my little son, now named Colin. He was lifeless, deep blue, and obviously stillborn. Seventeen minutes. It seemed over.

Slowly and in an understanding way, I patted the physician on his left shoulder and in a low voice quietly and sadly said to him, "It's all right, Doctor, the Lord gives and the Lord takes away— blessed be the name of the Lord."

My guess is the physician was not a follower of Jesus, because his reaction to what I said was one of shock—especially since he had just unsuccessfully battled for the life of this baby boy. He pulled away from me with disgust on his face, not saying a word, but saying everything with his contorted facial features.

As he abruptly turned toward me, he removed his hands from my stillborn son. At the very moment I quoted Scripture, the arched body of our little newborn released a gust of air that filled the room. The doctor jumped like a scared child, not able to believe what he had just seen.

Colin was alive and, as we found out later, completely healthy! My son was alive!

For the first time in my life as a godly man, I experienced the bitter fear of my Father's love. I originally had *hope*, then I was *hurt*, but God *intentionally* interrupted with *help*.

From here on out, I could be no less intentional in my own journey as a parent, especially since it worked the way I wanted it to work—or so I thought.

# Chapter Four

# Healthy Intentional Parenting

Healthy intentional parenting comes in many forms. Our family's favorite intentional family activity was and is our annual trip to Catalina Island.

For twenty-seven years we have been intentional about going each year to the Pacific Ocean, creating a tradition of vacationing where our spirits could be filled. Catalina Island is where we go. It is where our family's health has been renewed each year.

Santa Catalina Island is a wonderful slice of Heaven on Earth, just twenty-six miles off the coastline of Southern California. On that island rests a cove just two miles from the main city of Avalon. It's called Gallagher's Cove. Within that cove each summer resides a Christian family camp called Campus by the Sea (CBS). It is a strategically important place of rest, for our family and for many others.

Santa Catalina Island was made somewhat famous in the early 1960s by the Four Preps' Top 40 song "26 Miles (Santa Catalina)," which included lyrics such as "Twenty-six miles across the sea / Santa Catalina is a-waitin' for me. / Santa Catalina, the island of romance."

Our family's experience with Catalina had little to do with romance but much to do with bringing our family together, as Gary Smalley personally told me, "under crazy camping conditions in cabins and tents, experiencing life-changing events that no one wanted—but all ultimately enjoyed." Families can prosper in such planned-for chaos.

More recently, singer-songwriter Danny Oertli penned these lyrics about taking time to be with his family camping on the island of Santa Catalina in his song "Catalina":

CATALINA

© Danny Oertli

*Don't think twice*
*Take my hand tonight*
*You can hear the ship's last call*
*The lights of L.A.*
*Will all fade away*
*Catalina isn't far.*

*Stars shine clear*
*On the Pleasure Pier.*
*We can rent a boat at Joe's*
*Float on the waves*
*Where the dolphins play*
*All the way to Lover's Cove*
*And I'll see you there.*

*I'll be with you on Catalina*
*Oo, ou, ou, ou, ou, ou, ou*
*Skies are blue on Catalina*

*When I'm with you.*
*Kick back, relax*
*There's no turning back*
*Nowhere I'd rather be*
*Than here with you*
*And the seagulls, too*
*A little bit of heaven by the sea*
*Oh, it's not that far.*

Santa Catalina's Campus by the Sea offers all of that to our family, year after year, and now decade after decade. It was simply "not that far," as the song lyrics say.

Our longtime friends and mentors, Terry and Francie Bush, invited us on our first visit to the camp on Catalina Island.

Oh, and by the way, I *hated* camping. The bad memories I had of my dad taking our family on traditional camping trips did not make the decision easy to join these folks on Catalina. The thought of tents and fish lines and dirt and idleness all combined to make me initially not want to attend. My past experience showed me that parents seemed to always be angry during camping trips. General chaos ruled the day when, in my childhood, we transplanted the seven siblings and an angry mom. Though these rough-and-tumble times were my childhood experiences of camping, I would find that they had little to do with what we were about to experience.

We first attended CBS in 1987. Along with copious amounts of Coppertone, cumbersome beach chairs, and way too many clothes, we had two-year-old Meg and five-year-old Nate in tow. Not knowing what to expect, but hoping that a bit of the fabled and plush Fantasy Island might greet us, I was immediately let down when we exited the large boat. Catalina is a very hilly desert island. I was surprised to find out that each family shared the duties of cleaning up after dinner as an "opportunity to serve" and that the morning was reserved for Bible study and teaching. I remember sarcastically saying to myself, *Where's Ricardo Montalban, the host, and his sidekick from the* Fantasy Island *TV show?* thinking that somehow we had booked the wrong island.

Midweek during that first visit I concluded that although CBS was not quite the place for fun drinks with colorful umbrellas, we'd give it a try, anyway. And I'm glad we did. Something changed inside of me. I began to see God's fingerprints on the many families who served one another. I saw college staff helping little toddlers and high school kids sitting with their parents. From that day to now, we intentionally brought our kids to CBS every summer. It's been twenty-seven years so far, and it doesn't look like we'll soon be disconnecting from this tradition, now that our grandson loves the island, and now that we have a new granddaughter.

As children themselves, Nate, Meg, and later Colin each loved the fact that whatever else might change in their family's life— Dad's career, Mom's place of teaching, where we lived in California (or Idaho), where we would serve in Christian ministry—we'd always have Campus by the Sea on Catalina Island each summer. We were anchored to the Lord on the shores of that island camp.

Building intentional positive traditions, like we did with Campus by the Sea, was so helpful to our family. Nate loved that he could wander in the large cove's hills amid buffaloes, wild pigs, and all types of bugs and small lizards. He especially loved the beachfront with its beautiful rocky shore, the clear underwater ocean views during snorkeling, and the opportunity for the semi-scientific study of a prominent rock jetty that houses an amazing array of ocean life.

We saw our kids come alive on Catalina Island, as they participated in learning Scriptures, singing worship songs, and loving the Creator who had created all of this. Susan and I determined to intentionally bring our children back again and again to Catalina Island. The kids looked forward the entire year to being on Catalina Island each summer.

As the years progressed, we came to realize that being intentional in our parenting did not mean that the vacation would be without incident. One year Nate was found smoking up-canyon, in the middle of the dry brush, by the camp director, Paul Friesen. Paul had known Nate since he was six years old. Nonetheless, Paul clearly and forcefully told Nate that he would throw us out of camp if Nate's bad behavior continued. Nate obeyed on the outside but seethed on the inside. He was so angry; with clenched teeth he said in private to our family, "Why has Paul become such a mean jerk?" Susan and I were stunned by Nate's selfishness and surliness. We explained that Paul Friesen had always loved Nate and Nate had always loved Paul and obeyed him. "Paul hasn't changed, Nate, you have" was the only honest answer my wife could give. He was dumbfounded and shut his mouth. It was a powerful lesson for all of us. Nate agreed to obey the terms Paul set down. Paul Friesen and his wife, Virginia, allowed us to stay at the camp with the clear understanding that we'd be asked to leave if Nate broke his pledge that summer.

In the years to come, Nate reached the full stature of his young manhood under the palm trees and surrounded by the sound of surf splashing against the rocks of the island's shoreline, learning about Christ, and helping people. His last visit with us on the island was the summer after he graduated from high school in 2000. Nine years later, near the end of Nate's life, when he and I both thought we'd still have decades of time together to revisit and enjoy Catalina Island, he remarked to me how "next year I'd like to come to CBS with you; do you think that's possible, Dad?" My answer was, "Yes, Nate, we'd be honored to have you with us again on Catalina Island." Those words are even more meaningful to me in the summers that have passed since Nate's death. Intentional parenting means planning to have a purposeful and meaningful life together, especially when obedience is at the heart of such fun.

## Purchasing a Life, Not Just a House

Families do not always have the luxury of purchasing the home of their dreams. We certainly did not. But what we did have was the option of choosing where we lived and what type of street we lived on. As our kids began to grow we determined that we needed a bigger home. Susan loved the idea of buying a home on a cul-de-sac, so that our kids could play in the front yard, run in the street, and enjoy other neighborhood friends. She spent many wonderful childhood years on such a street in Glendora, California. We therefore purposefully decided to live in a neighborhood with a cul-de-sac and made a firm decision not to settle for less. In short order we bought a home on a cul-de-sac in a brand-new neighborhood chock-full of little kids around our children's ages. Our kids loved the freedom afforded them by running and playing in that neighborhood, even building a go-cart and racing it endlessly around and around in the circle of pavement, engaging in Idaho's winter pasttime sport of snowball fights from snow forts, and walking to a neighborhood store for popcorn.

Being intentional also meant being flexible in moving to a different home when the children grew even older. As the little-kid years receded, we knew that junior high and high school would soon be upon us, with all of the complexities of new friends, dating, and cars. I returned to memories of my own high school years in West Covina, California, at a home my dad moved us to that had a pool—certainly not unusual for a Southern California home. Armed with the knowledge of how fun a home with a pool could be, we sought a home that either already had a pool or had space enough for us to build one. We were intentional in what we looked for, and when we walked into one particular home, I could tell by my preteenage daughter's body language that this was the one. It had a big backyard, but no pool. So we built one! And the memories started immediately with the first shovelful of dirt as the pool was constructed. It is a wonderful home with many great memories throughout the teen years of our three kids. We came to understand that one of the secrets to life is simply enjoying the turning of time's hands.

## The Value of Having Pets

We always had family pets. Animals seemed to be in family snapshots from the beginning. Cats came and went, snakes and gerbils populated the glass aquariums. But it was always dogs that filled our hearts with the most warmth. Our appreciation of canines began one year into our marriage—we found a puppy and named her Cinnamon. She stayed with us for ten years. As new canines joined us over the years, we returned to the spice rack several more times for additional names: Spicey, Sugar, Honey, and, most recently, Cocoa. The kids were given the duty of naming each dog, knowing that Nutmeg was never quite an option! In almost three and a half decades we have always had a dog. Pets taught our three children responsibility and unconditional love, providing wonderful memories over their childhood years. As Nate and Meg grew to adulthood, their love of dogs continued. Becoming dog owners themselves, they chose, however, to abandon the spice rack for names, since Thyme and Cumin just didn't seem right for their dogs! In Colin's junior year in high school (and just months after Nate died), Colin's dog Cocoa began experiencing terrible pain in her eyes. The visit to the vet was agonizing for us. Cocoa was diagnosed with glaucoma—an eye disease so severe and painful in dogs that the doctor suggested we put her down. "Are there any other options?" Colin and Susan asked the vet. There was one option but it seemed so severe: surgery to remove the dog's eyes. As a family, we discussed this option, with all its long-term responsibilities and repercussions. Colin would soon be going off to college at the United States Military Academy at West Point, leaving Susan and me with a blind dog. We counted the costs, kept Cocoa alive by having the surgery done, and began our new journey in life traveling with a sightless dog who now seems to love us even more than she did in the past. Cocoa may think of us as a dog's best friends for how we helped her, but my guess is we get the better end of the bargain. Saving her life when our own son had just died allowed us to appreciate the love of a pet even more.

## Spotting the Lie

At the core of film and television is the concept of scripted lines. Nothing is spoken in a theatrical presentation that does not have a worldview. And not all worldviews are equal. Intentional parenting allowed us the opportunity to tackle this reality head-on. Earning money always motivated our three kids. Susan and I determined that whenever a lie was spotted in a TV show, we would pay a nickel to the child who saw it. We had movie nights and played "spot the lie" from messages delivered in films or TV shows that were in opposition to our family's standards. At first it was a slow process and required some prodding from Susan and me. But as Nate and Meg realized they would instantly receive a nickel for their piggy banks, they began to pay more and more attention to the lines delivered on TV shows and VHS tapes. It became commonplace to hear Nate, Meg, and later Colin yell out in the middle of a program, "I spot the lie!"

## Nathan the Adventurer

Bedtime stories were told every night. Every night. Certainly books were read and reread. I honestly can't tell you how many thousands of times I read "Cinderella" to our first two kids! But then one night, I had an inspiration—I asked Nate to choose five items in his bedroom for inclusion in a story. As he listed those items to me, I began the first ad-libbed story of a character I named Nathan the Adventurer. The tale was a wondrous story of intrigue, travel, and adventure. Interwoven in the fabric of the story suddenly was the first item he selected, then his second and third. But when it came time for his fourth and fifth items to be included, I turned to Nate, motioning for him to continue with the tale, saying, "And . . ." It was at this point in time that a family tradition of nighttime stories of Nathan the Adventurer, Megan the Adventurer, and Colin the Adventurer all started. We told nightly stories of glory and high intrigue—together. Years later, this would prove to be something that reclaimed a space in Nate's memory when he was a prisoner in solitary confinement.

## School and Sports

Part of intentional parenting also involves school and sports. As Christian parents in the 1980s we were influenced again by our college friends Leah and John VanderWende, who were much more mature Christians than we. Leah and John invited us to their church to watch a film series called Focus on the Family by a USC-trained psychologist, Dr. James Dobson. We enjoyed his homespun humor and his stories and his commitment to helping young people like us raise families in a balanced Christian way. He became important not only to us but to an entire generation of young families.

A few years later, Leah handed us a Focus on the Family audiotape that dealt with an issue called "home education"; the tape was an interview between Dr. Dobson and Dr. Raymond Moore, the father of home education in America.

It was intriguing to listen as Dr. Moore spoke of how parents were "the natural teachers to their children." The more I listened, the more I liked what I heard. Somewhere in the interview I heard the term "homeschool" for the first time. The term itself sounded somewhat Amish to me, yet Dr. Dobson was agreeing with his guest, and because of my experience with Dr. Dobson, I trusted that Focus on the Family would not have an oddball on their show, intentionally or unintentionally misguiding young fathers and mothers like us. Many of us trusted our family's life to Focus on the Family and what they taught.

So, we listened, and when the tape was over, we listened again. Homeschooling seemed like a legitimate alternative for us.

I tend to have a contrarian perspective on American culture, in that whatever seems currently to be in fashion to people, I find to be boring or useless. This perspective seemed to foster my worldview of going in a different faith direction when we became born-again followers of Jesus. I looked at Susan and stated very emphatically, "If regular culture is not homeschooling, then there must be something beneficial for us if we *do* homeschool!" And we did.

Over the years, I've come to conclude that the phrase "contrarian perspective" is just a euphemism for possibly being rebellious—which, in a real way, we were when it came to our children's education. Many in the homeschool community embrace this rebellion and simply call it "alternative education." Being active in it for two decades plus, we have changed our perspective, depending on the specific offshoot of the homeschooling movement. Homeschooling has been widely embraced by the secular community as well. It appears that the child-centered nature of modern America has become naturally enamored with the homeschool movement.

Little did I know at the time that we would homeschool for the next twenty-four years of our lives, finding ourselves initially as pioneers in the movement, ultimately graduating two of our three children via a home education curriculum.

Though we educated our kids at home, we also believed in preschool, private school, and public school. Susan had been a public elementary school teacher in the early days of our marriage. Today she remains a public school teacher as well.

Nate was attending Christian preschool at the time we first explored home education. We decided not to reenroll him for the following year, but not without one final significant moment in Nate's little life as a six-year-old preschooler. It was a moment that has stayed with us ever since—and one that I mentioned in my eulogy of him.

One day after I picked him up from the preschool, Nate looked at me, paused, and then dramatically told me, "Dad, I'm gonna send a sofa on ahead."

Puzzled, I asked what he meant.

He said, "Daddy, the Bible says we have mansions in Heaven and that Jesus went ahead to make 'em ready for us. So, whenever we show love, in Jesus' name, it's like we send a sofa on ahead. You know, to fix up our mansion, one thing at a time—for when we get there."

I couldn't argue with his theology. "Sending a sofa on ahead" seemed the right thing to do.

As a family we began sending sofas on ahead, supporting missionaries in need, mentoring families, giving from our hearts, purposefully living our lives out loud.

Nate initiated this in our family. We still give in those same areas today. His little-boy voice still questioningly cries out to me today, "Are we *still* sending sofas on ahead?"

Early on we recognized the importance of mission trips and role models along with significant adults in our kids' lives. Many godly men and women came into our kids' lives at key points. We appreciated their quiet talks with our kids, their interest in each child's life and interests, and how each adult lived his or her life out loud with our children watching. The Gospel was apparent, even when words were absent.

Nate's Christian education gave way to public school in ninth grade. He wanted desperately to transition from a religious school environment to a secular school. Little did we know what was about to hit us.

Those years were not easy for him, since we were well known

in the community and the goals I had worked for were not always in tandem with then current leaders of the National Education Association in our state. Nate was negatively singled out by certain teachers. He seemed to thrive on the conflict, and yet he questioned whether the things we'd taught him were as real as we thought they were. Doubt crept in, as it does for many teenagers during transition times.

Nate loved spending time with his best friend, Mark Smit. From fourth grade on, these two boys were inseparable. Mark's parents, Paul and Diane Smit, were significant adults in Nate's life. They opened their home to our son from the early years of elementary school through his time in college. He was loved and received there. Mark and Nate were brothers of the heart.

## Encouraging Relationships with Significant Adults

During this time, Nate sought the mentoring of Russ Fulcher, a local businessman and friend of our family. Russ hired Nate to work around his small Idaho farm, engaged Nate in conversation, and encouraged my son to be involved in politics. Nate agreed to be involved politically. Russ and his family invited Nate and our family to Idaho's gorgeous skiing resort area, Sun Valley, on a number of occasions. They'd often blow past my level of skiing and end up on the black diamonds high in the peaks of this near-heavenly skiing terrain. Russ would ask Nate questions about life, and Nate would often vent—especially as he grew into his teen years. The key to it was that Nate sought the friendship of a significant adult and received it from Russ.

It was during these tough high school years that Nate helped run the literature drops in several Idaho state legislative races—

with his candidates winning all of them. He couldn't believe he was getting paid to help put conservatives into office. Russ was proud of Nate, and Nate loved Russ. It was a wonderful thing to watch as a dad.

Years later, when Nate passed away, the speaker of the Idaho House of Representatives, Representative Lawerence Denney; the majority leader of the Idaho House, Representative Mike Moyle; several other representatives; a former U.S. congressman; former U.S. representative Bill Sali; and one state senator came to either his viewing or his funeral. The state senator? Senator Russ Fulcher—elected since Nate had gone to prison. Nate's one regret in politics, he told me, was not being able to help Russ win his race. Maybe Nate's gift of getting people elected might have rubbed off on Russ without any of us even knowing it!

For Nate, sports were also an outlet to share the good news of Christ. A longtime friend of mine, Steve Switzer, loved Nate as if he were his own son. I attribute Nate's lifelong enjoyment of sports and sports trivia to Steve. Somehow, Nate and Steve were on the same frequency about national sports, professional sports, sports radio shows, and the individual lives of athletes—which I was not. Politics was my area of interest.

I do remember how Nate developed a keen interest in Ken Griffey, Jr., after asking me to take him to a farm-team baseball game in San Bernardino when we lived in Southern California. Steve apparently told Nate that Griffey would be a "comer" and that Nate would soon see this outfielder for the San Bernardino Spirit play in the big leagues. Nate listened to Steve. I listened to Nate. And we went to see a teenage version of Ken Griffey, Jr., play ball.

Sure enough, Nate retrieved one of Ken Griffey's first professionally hit home run balls from the parking lot behind the semipro field, and he was hooked on "Junior" as he made his way to the Seattle Mariners and on into the history books of Major League Baseball.

Nate and Steve maintained a solid friendship, with Steve helping him out financially at times, unbeknownst to me; whenever Nate faced some big obstacle or two and I wasn't in the loop or couldn't help, Steve was there for Nate, and these two friends loved Jesus.

When Nate died, Steve Switzer called our daughter and told her that he was paying for Nate's funeral. He said he "had to do it." His love for our son was that deep.

At Nate's viewing we placed baseball cards of Ken Griffey, Jr., and the Seattle Mariners along with pennants and mementos all around his casket. Steve couldn't bear to see Nate's body at the viewing, but he sat with my family during the funeral and wept with us.

Not enough can be said about how intentional parenting works. Providing the opportunity for significant adults in our children's lives allows the young adults to grow in ways we as parents may not always be able to foster. It's part of intentional parenting, and it's nothing to be afraid of.

Significant adult Christian friends like the Smits, Steve Switzer, and Russ Fulcher encouraged godly freedom for our children through faith, and that is especially important when we parent out of fear-based concerns—which stands in complete opposition to walking in faith. And without faith it is impossible to please God.

Steve put it to me this way:

*Dennis,*

*For some reason, Nate had a hard time dealing with all of the love that was around him. It was not that he was trying to live up to you or your expectations. Instead, I believe, from my view in the cheap seats, he could not find a reason why he was so worthy. One needs to look around and see all of the turmoil with his peers, their parents, divorce, cheating, etc. Instead, he was blessed with a rock for a father and a near saint for a mother. With Colin, he [also] saw himself, and was so proud of him.*

*From there, he started to identify with those kids who did not have what he had—unconditional love. He found the good in those people, and could not understand why he was blessed and they were not. It was then that he started to try and identify with them, which led to the experiments with drugs. That road, once started upon, became too difficult for him to detour from. The power of drugs on the self-conscious is undeniable. I can only guess what his motives were. But I know what they were not. His heart, his soul, his love for you were solid. He was not searching for himself any more or less than any other kid, including us, at that age. He knew who he was. He was not rebelling against you and Sue—it was not his nature.*

*Your friend,*
*Steve*

*P.S.: You say that I have always been there for you and your family. The power of your faith has helped me more times and in more ways than I can ever express.*

Love overpowers sin and fear. And fear-based parenting grieves the very heart of God and achieves nothing but sorrow, as Susan and I learned to our deep sadness.

# Chapter Five

# Fear-Based Parenting

Fear-based parenting is a cancer that has attacked the body of Christ. Nothing positive comes from it. Nothing.

I know, because I often parented that way. Not always, but often enough to create tension throughout the years with my wife and my children—especially Nate.

Those who practice it generally do so with a set of rules that would make even the strictest first-century Pharisee proud.

Fear-based parenting comes in two forms: the fear of what others think of us as parents, and the fear of the harm that might come to our children and the evil that can affect them.

## *The Fear of What Others Think*

My children figured out rather quickly that I would not discipline them when we were at a church service or some other Christian event. Our children's poor behavior in public was often overlooked because of my fear of looking bad. Contrary to logic, I allowed chaos to reign because it was easier to correct the behavior later, while out of view of onlookers, than it was to face the fear of looking bad in others' eyes as it happened. You may be nodding your head in an understanding that comes from experience; you may also be agreeing with me about my hypocrisy. My kids would now say that I often acted out of fear. Our children tend to know us, don't they? They know when our lack of discipline is based on fear and hypocrisy.

What would your children say about you?

A lot of parental fear stems from an oddly held sense of comparison. Many evangelical Christians never say the word, but it's there in conversations with fellow church members and family: competition. Like boxers sizing up opponents from across the ring or high school teens measuring their competitors, the look is always the same: "How good a person are you? How good am I?" It's a sick sort of fleshly comparison. One family's troubled ADD gonzo kid is quickly compared with another person's compliant child, and a religiously supported pecking order of value seems to happen naturally. It is unhealthy and yet it is there. After many years, we saw that unhealthy behavior in ourselves.

*"How good a person are you? How good am I?" It's a sick sort of fleshly comparison.*

For example, among some evangelicals the idea of testing children for attention deficit disorder and ADHD is not even a possibility. Unstated but seemingly implied by not a few Christian leaders and pastors is that if you test your child for ADD or ADHD, you are admitting that you cannot handle your own child. My own experience shows that examining possible medical solutions to ADD/ADHD poses a deep threat to many parents within the Christian community.

## The Fear of Danger Affecting Our Children

For many years Susan and I, without meaning to, raised our family with fear-based parenting—fear of what might happen to them and fear of the evil that might influence them.

Whether evangelical Christianity of the 1980s directed us to do so or not, we chose to live in fear. Concern about the harm and evil that could befall our children was deeply intrusive and yet was accepted by so many Christian parents. This fear-based parenting gripped the hearts of many Christian parents. It still does today.

Susan and I were no exception. For example, we were crippled with fear when we learned about a little boy named Adam Walsh. Along with many other parents, Susan and I bore the scars of a wound we never personally endured.

Adam Walsh was a Little Leaguer in Hollywood, Florida. His mother and father, like so many parents, loved their son and poured themselves into his life, his activities, and his future. His father, John Walsh, was a businessman and his mother, Revé Walsh, was a homemaker.

On July 27, 1981, Revé decided to take Adam with her to the local Sears. While Mom looked at this sale or that special, she left her boy for seven minutes. He busied himself at the video counter with some older, more rambunctious boys. Security guards soon threw the boys out of the store, including Adam.

The terribly swift collision between two unfixable actions then occurred.

Adam disappeared from the entrance of the store without a trace. Adam's story became a book and then a television motion picture. What happened to Adam sparked the creation of John Walsh's TV show *America's Most Wanted.*

John and Revé Walsh's story of the kidnapping of their firstborn child burned its imprint into the minds of parents across America.

At kitchen tables throughout the country, sadness greeted many morning meals. It seemed every half gallon of milk suddenly had Adam's face on it. Eventually thousands of other children appeared on milk cartons, day after day, bowl after bowl, year after year.

They were the faces of precious little children who had been abducted and whose fate was in the balance. I could hardly pour the milk on my kids' Cheerios without convulsively shivering from fear.

The unwanted fearful reviewing of each child victim's story left me scared—nearly petrified. I prayed for the best in my own kids' lives and worried about the worst for the families of those kids. Staring at me, morning after morning, were little kidnapped kids who were born in the same years as my children. At that time, I unintentionally struggled with whether my fear was real and justified, or whether it was a manifestation of my deep fear of losing my own young children. I didn't want to think about it, yet I continued to obsess over the safety of my children.

Eventually they found Adam Walsh's severed head. The pain of the known facts deeply fed the fear of the unknown in countless parents across America. It was the fear of the horrific possibilities that was the most painful for parents. The possibilities were real and ever present. And they could come to pass with any or all of my children.

My greatest fear quickly became the death of my own child.

From the first journal entry a few weeks after Nate was born—

and, ironically a single day after Adam's disappearance— I penned my fear of loss in Nate's baby book:

*My greatest fear quickly became the death of my own child.*

*July 28, 1981*
*In your goals and desires, keep paramount the question: Is what I am doing pleasing to God. Don't worry about Mom and Dad, we're pleased that God even loaned you to us.*

The words were telling and prophetic: "even loaned you to us." From that first journal comment until Nate's death, almost three decades later, I journaled, nearly daily. These many years later, I am able to see how fearful I was of losing my children, beginning with my firstborn. As I write this book, what would have been Nate's thirty-first birthday has occurred. Even these decades later I can still experience that desperate and fearful feeling in the pit of my stomach as I remember what it felt like when he was a baby and I was so utterly afraid of him being kidnapped and killed.

Much of what we did with Nate and Meg was founded in fear-based parenting. We were fearful for them on many levels: for example, the simple act of our children playing outside our own house in Southern California prompted the perpetual fear of them being kidnapped.

The fear of death held us tightly in its grasp and eventually became more real as Nate's life spiraled downward. Through his use of illegal drugs and a long series of flawed decisions, Nate chose paths that ultimately and unintentionally led to his death. And when he finally died, at the age of twenty-seven, our family convulsed, I am sure, with much the same deep sadness that the Walshes endured at the loss of their son Adam. Both had killers.

We were also fearful of what our children watched on TV, so we made PBS the only station they could view. We were fearful of the rental movies they watched, so we rigged up Curse Free TV (a system by which curse words were predetected, eliminated, and then substituted with other words). Our kids still watched TV but spent much of their time trying to figure out which curse words were being eliminated. What an exercise in futility it was!

## Rules Without Relationship

Josh McDowell, international youth speaker and member of Campus Crusade for Christ, said it best years ago: "Rules without relationship equal rebellion." His words ring truer with each decade that passes.

Christians who implement fear-based parenting tend to believe a lie: they believe that because their child is obeying their commands, he or she is getting better and better. But such parents—and I was one of them—are merely fooling themselves. Could it be that you are fooling yourself? Your child may be sitting down on the outside but standing up on the inside, fist clenched and screaming with all he or she has: "Why won't you listen to me?" Fear-based parents within the Christian evangelical community seldom really listen.

Even so, the importance of rules cannot be overstated. They *are* important; everywhere from the Department of Motor Vehicles to the U.S. military services to business and finance, rules allow us to live in order and in community.

Though relationships within the larger forms of culture, such as in the military, may not demand intimacy, there is a clear sense of positional authority among and between the involved individuals, such as when a sergeant salutes a captain, or a captain salutes a brigadier general.

Time after time, culture after culture, rules have helped us achieve more as a civilization because we implement them in our most common denominator: the family. As the family is ordered, so goes society. In a family environment, intimacy is key. Positional authority may hold a certain amount of importance for children as they face their parents, but the deeper things of life involve the loving relationship between a child who knows he or she is loved and parents who love them. Mutual, loving, and caring relationships foster the administration and implementation of necessary rules.

The natural void that occurs as a result of rules without relationship is something akin to the emptiness of the Law alone. The Old Testament's clear construction of the Law showed that man understood what was being asked of him. There was no misunderstanding of what was being asked and what was being provided as potential solutions. God's chosen people saw the need for the Ten Commandments and ultimately understood the need for the 613 additional laws that followed. But many of the people lacked relationship with God, and thus their obedience left much to be desired.

Because they understood the Law, that did not mean they obeyed it. The Law alone could not change hearts. A change of heart comes with a relationship with God and ultimately with Jesus Christ.

I tended to parent our first two children with a set of rules and regulations—some stated, some subtle. My children knew what the tone of my voice and the look in my eyes meant. And they learned to fear it, sometimes obeying on the outside but rebelling on the inside.

As a little boy, when Nate felt angry, he tended to cover up his emotions because he believed that I knew it all as a godly father. In a real way I encouraged this outward compliance. I did not always give him the freedom to express his feelings; I came to believe that quietness meant compliance. And I was wrong.

> *I came to believe that quietness meant compliance. And I was wrong.*

Controlling my own passions when family rules were disobeyed was extremely difficult for me. I saw each infraction by my son as a personal assault against what Susan and I were structuring as our family's plan. Nate seemed out of control and always challenging my authority, even from a very young age.

## Making Important Changes

Rather than being self-obsessed and too concerned about how we looked as parents, Susan and I slowly learned to start becoming students of our children. We knew that what we were doing as parents was only having a limited positive effect, and we decided to be more intentional in our parenting and less child-centered. In one sense, we became more intent on reshaping our children's will without breaking their hearts.

The tightly interwoven strands of intentionality and child-centeredness began to unravel as we gained more accurate information, but it was very difficult.

Gary Chapman's book *The Five Love Languages* helped us understand why we were not succeeding at telling one another that we loved one another. We gained insight into why, at times, we were so upset and angry when our expectations were unmet. Gary writes that every person perceives love through one or more of five love languages. Problems arise when we try "speaking" love to another person in *our* love language instead of his or hers.

The five languages are:

1. Gifts
2. Words of encouragement
3. Physical touch
4. Quality time
5. Acts of service

All of us "speak" some portion of these languages. The key is to be a student of your family members and center in on *their* greatest love languages—then speak those languages to them. Buy Gary's book and become students of your kids and grandkids.

My principle love language involves words of encouragement. Nate's involved spending quality time together.

There were so many times when I would encourage Nate, telling him that he could accomplish whatever he put his mind to. I attempted to speak words of encouragement into him, but his reaction was bitterly negative. I learned later that he believed I was not being honest with him about his limitations.

On the other hand, Nate would want to have quality time with me, and I would simply blow him off because I had business to do or other children to attend to. We were like two trains in the night going in opposite directions. We eventually learned that Nate's love language was *not* words of encouragement, the language that I'd used for years on him. Rather, his language was quality time.

As we learned more, we both began to change how we talked to each other—which brought about much greater communication and deeper intimacy.

When Nate and Meg were out of high school, I had our entire family take the DISC Behavioral Assessment, and I was able to see clear patterns of positive and negative behavior and unveil other crucial answers. It was as if I had stumbled on what my kids' behaviors *really* were. It wasn't a matter of their attitude; rather, it was a matter of how they experienced life. I was both utterly thrilled by what I learned and deeply saddened that it had taken so long for me to find out. Please visit TTIFamilyFirst.com and have each of your family members take the assessment. It may be life changing.

It was as if I had been handed keys that easily slipped into the fear-based parenting locks and watched as the chains fell away; the insights showed me how to embrace my children's hearts. This was intentional parenting at its best.

My only echoing cry was: *Why did it take me so long to find this out?*

# Chapter Six

# Choosing Safe Friends

Being deliberate in our own friend-
ships with parents seemed helpful in our early child-rearing days.
Many of our friendship links came as a result of church relationships or homeschool groups. At times, my employment served us
with opportunities to meet new friends and their children.

For many young parents, the network of their kids' sports teams,
music groups, and school activities opens up avenues for them to
meet new friends. The difficult part of developing new friends is
that it can take some time before we as parents determine if those
new family friends are "good" or "bad" for us. But friendships usually just happen, without any sense of deliberate direction.

## Always on the Lookout

As a result of our fear-based parenting, even with these newfound
friendships, I was always on the lookout for possible attacks against

my children's innocence or the adoption by my kids of some naughty new words. Over and over again, I looked for exterior signs of attack and rebellion—when it happened I often placed blame on the friend or his or her parent. The nature of scared and fearful parents is that they create an atmosphere in which their children often fail to accept responsibility for what they did that was wrong. We as parents do our children a disservice when we blame scapegoats for our children's wrongdoing. We unknowingly create an atmosphere of excuses. We may not see it, but our children do.

Though I was quite aware of my son's sin nature as a little boy, there were many times where I simply sought to place the blame for a certain behavior problem on another child. Fear has a way of doing that. As a parent I found it nearly impossible to be watchful without being fearful. I chose my friends carefully and allowed our kids to play with theirs. I so longed for a protected environment for my children that at times I was too lenient in examining my new friends for possibilities of danger.

*As a parent I found it nearly impossible to be watchful without being fearful.*

In Southern California, our family developed a neighborly relationship with a family who lived near us. We had playful water fights with them, stretching hoses and tossing water balloons. Since we had a swimming pool, we invited the kids over to go swimming and served them poolside snacks when they took us up on our offer.

The relationship advanced further. We invested time in the neighboring children, asked about their future, and got to know about their high school days. We enjoyed them and helped their family whenever we could with landscaping or other manual labor needs that would occasionally pop up.

It was a budding friendship and an opportunity for the other children to care about my children. My thick walls of protective fear-based parenting opened to allow this family into our lives.

Until something terrible happened.

## *Fears Realized*

One fall evening when Nate was five years old, our neighbor, who was visiting our home, said, "Just have Nate come over to my house and my teenage son will watch him."

We trusted her. We trusted him. We should not have done so.

Months later, while Nate and I were driving alone in my truck, Nate asked me, "Daddy, why is my peepee shaped different than our neighbor's?"

It is hard, these many years later, to adequately construct sentences that portray my internal reaction of rage to this innocently asked question. I gripped the steering wheel in terror, white-knuckling it while I slowly asked him to repeat his question. I then tried to answer his question in a tone that wouldn't alarm him.

All my greatest fears were about to be realized. Like a self-justified argument, my fear-based parenting seemed to shout out, "See, I told you!"

*I gripped the steering wheel in terror, white-knuckling it while I slowly asked him to repeat his question.*

"Well, Nate, what does *his* peepee look like?" was all I could force out of my constricted throat. Nate began to describe in his five-year-old way the difference between circumcision and noncircumcision. I was instantly volcanic. I wanted to find that neighbor boy and kill him.

I asked for the particulars and found out that on the evening of a recent political event, the "trusted" neighbor boy had taken my innocent little five-year-old boy into his upstairs garage clubhouse and shown him pornography, ultimately displaying his adolescent genitals to my son.

My anger was white-hot. Here I had finally trusted someone—a neighbor—and had allowed a slight opening in the thick wall of protectionism, and perversion had immediately defiled the trust. It is one of the rare times in my life that I *really* wanted to kill another human being.

Returning home, I conferred with my wife and we determined to deal directly with the teenager. I demanded his presence at my house, took him in the backyard, and asked him face-to-face. I barely held my rage in check. He immediately crumpled, spilling his guts and begging me not to tell his mother. I gave him twenty-four hours to tell her, or I would.

The next day came and went, and the teen failed to comply, so my wife and I met with the boy's mother. It was a terrible moment for us, and it was a terrible moment for trust. Unmoved, the woman defended her son, and we agreed to meet again the next day. With the turning of each day, I could not even look at our neighbor's house without a sense of wrenching in my soul. I was disgusted with her son's behavior, and I was disgusted with myself. I felt I should have acted on my impulse and caused great pain to the porn-addicted teen. I felt I had let my son down by not being there either to protect him or violently defend him.

The final discussion we had with the mother was short and simple. Her son admitted he showed his genitals but that "nothing else happened." We were wrong in bringing it forward and making it a big deal, she felt.

Nothing else happened? Really? How about this: innocence was attacked and trust was eviscerated.

Yet, ultimately, I chose not to call the police and have him arrested, because of my concern about turning a mere fifteen-year-old with foolish porn-addicted behavior into a registered lifelong sex offender.

In choosing not to act, I ultimately felt that I had failed my own boy. The clashing and chaotic emotions were almost too much for me to bear. Nate had been violated, that was certain, yet he had not been sexually molested by the teen. This is how I justified my decision to not turn the boy in to the authorities. Years later, after working with hundreds of sex offenders in our county jail, I came to understand that the best thing I could have done was to turn that fifteen-year-old in. I regret my decision to this day.

*I'm not certain I grew wiser, but I did grow more fearful.*

Regret is a painful and at times debilitating emotion. At other times, regret actually forces us to deal with something we did poorly and overcome it, so that the next time something like it happens, we can rest on our past experience and do what is wiser. In this case, I'm not certain I grew wiser, but I did grow more fearful.

I started being extremely careful about allowing our children to have *any* outside relationships. Everyone became a possible violator. I became even more fearful and decided that my family needed to be protected from the chance of further attacks.

## Positive Role Models

There was, however, one group of folks whom I loved and with whom my children were in complete safety.

During those years, I was a partner in a construction hydroseeding company. My partner, Willis "Woody" Wood, had many large-scale projects that demanded time and attention. Our labor force was made up of thirty or forty Mexican laborers—all caring family men who were thousands of miles away from their wives and children. They adopted my then two kids as though they were their own.

It was not uncommon for me to take one or both of my children with me to construction job sites. The kids loved being with me, and I loved having them around as I supervised laborers, inspected sites, and took the kids out to breakfast and lunch. They rode shotgun with me, and to this day, fond memories have been shared about those times.

During those many trips, I'd keep the car radio music to a minimum so that the kids and I could talk. On some trips, we'd take a foreman, Lupe Corona, with us in the work truck. Lupe did not speak English and ended up becoming our family's Spanish teacher. He's been our friend now for thirty years. Both in the truck cab and on the job site, Lupe would point out different things and give their Spanish names to the kids.

Nate's love of Lupe and the other workers with our company met a need within him. Somehow the vulnerability of these men who only spoke Spanish was something he could understand—even at such a young age. He saw them as underdogs—unable to accomplish what others born in the United States had accomplished.

Twice during Nate's childhood, Lupe's family invited us to Tecomán, Mexico, to enjoy several weeks of living in their town. Nate made fast friends with Lupe's sons and their cousins. His appreciation for people who had nothing material yet had an abundance of love impacted him deeply.

My business partner, Woody Wood, held a special place in Nate's life as well. His daughter, Amber, was Nate's age, so Woody and Amber cared for my son as though he was a part of their family. Amber and Nate had a very special childhood friendship—unlike anything I have seen since. She brought out the fun and excitement in him, acknowledging his gifts, even as toddlers and then again as elementary school kids. It was a healthy friendship and one that allowed each child to be "better" just by being together. Woody's love for Nate was that of an uncle. He'd show Nate how to make things or how to handle tools. Woody treated Nate as a young man, even when my son was a mere boy. You could see in Nate's eyes that he was proud to be around Woody.

In addition, we enjoyed the deep friendship of Henri and Pam Raynaud. Henri has been the photographer to the stars within the evangelical community because of his long-standing friendship with the late Dr. Bill Bright and his decades of service to Campus Crusade for Christ.

Henri's formal portraits of our family included Nate as a toddler. The Raynauds had children in tandem with us—Janine and Kristin became like sisters to Nate and Meg. The depth of friendship with the Raynauds was at a level felt by each member of our family. This type of love and care cannot be fully and adequately presented in brief statements here. Some of Henri's portraits are included in this book—they paint a fullness of laughter and love that transcends words.

Family, too, was a great source of friendship for our kids. I come from a family of seven siblings and Susan comes from a family of five siblings. Aunts and uncles were a big part of our children's lives. Years later, when Nate passed away, all but one of his aunts and uncles were able to attend his service and show their love for

Nate. The one who could not attend later sent dear words of comfort to me. Nate's was a love that they, too, felt to their core. His maternal grandparents embraced him and loved him deeply.

One of the oddest friendships that deeply impacted Nate's life was with my father, Bill Mansfield. My dad is a World War II–era, Korean War, and Vietnam War–era veteran. He's tough as nails, always has been. Somehow Nate and his "Grand Pa" became close friends throughout all of his arrests, convictions, and imprisonment. They had things in common that I did not share with my dad. How a career military man and a drug addicted young man ever became the best of friends, I will never know, but love drew them together. And I loved it.

Nate felt the love of these friends to his core.

## A Newer, Safer Place

Despite everything that was comfortable and safe in the enclaves of close family and friends, I was still very fearful as a result of my perceptions of the California culture. It was as if the kidnappings, drug abuse, and gang violence were in our own backyard—almost in our own home.

After a time, I felt we needed to escape the whole Southern California busyness of life. I determined to move our family away from the very place where Nate wanted to stay. At ten years of age, Nate saw his world slipping away.

I placed our California residence for sale and sold my business. It took time. Nate was stubborn in not wanting to move. He became belligerent as we prepared to leave, and his anger at us became white-hot when we did move.

I was looking for a newer, safer place to live, despite his protestations.

But where should we move? Maybe we'd choose a place whose unofficial motto at the time was: "Idaho *is* what America *was.*"

*Chapter Seven*

# Focus on the Family

I never looked in my rearview mirror when I left California.

Though the planning took us a while, the actual move from California to Idaho came about as a result of one short article by a writer/editor named Chuck Donovan in the Focus on the Family public policy magazine, *Citizen*. We'd long been subscribers to the various magazines that Focus produced, but the *Citizen* magazine, in particular, had a fearless quality about it that we liked. Dr. James Dobson launched the magazine with the intent of creating a watchdog periodical that would allow national leaders and local public policy experts to express their concerns.

## *The Moral Majority and the Christian Coalition*

At the time, most of America was aware of the conservative Christian community's very vigorous long-term attempts to influence politics through nonprofit organizations. Both Jerry Falwell's Moral Majority and Pat Robertson's Christian Coalition counted the rich and powerful of the conservative community among their friends. Ronald Reagan spoke often of how Dr. Falwell's efforts were key to coalescing the faith-based conservative community throughout the United States.

Begun prior to 1979, the Moral Majority was viewed as the agent of change that ironically swept from the presidency a highly visible born-again Christian, Jimmy Carter, and replaced him with a neoconservative, Ronald Reagan. The Christian Coalition started not too long after that.

Jimmy Carter openly stated that he was born-again. In answer to a question of his faith during a later presidential debate, Ronald Regan said, "Am I a born-again Christian? Well, where I came from, we never used that term. I was born with my faith in God." And Dr. Falwell and Dr. Robertson built much of their organizations on the shoulders of the movement that President Reagan encouraged.

## Focus on the Family

Dr. James Dobson was different.

Though Dr. Dobson knew Ronald Reagan and admired him, Focus on the Family centered most of its early work in the late 1970s not on the personalities of conservative politicians or public policy issues, not on public policy areas of concern for new families, but on how to deal with a strong-willed child, how to help stop bed-wetting, how a couple might dare to discipline their kids, that sort of thing. It wasn't until 1990 that Dr. Dobson decided to enter into the public policy arena in a very systematic and well-organized way. Dr. Falwell welcomed him.

It was in 1990 when my bride called my attention to a Focus on the Family *Citizen* magazine article that Donovan wrote; she suggested that I consider calling Focus and making myself available to them in the worthwhile enterprise proposed in the article.

It said that Dr. Dobson and his staff desired to set up family-friendly Family Policy Councils in many states throughout the union. Rather than working in areas that would be seen as "political" (with candidates and electioneering), Focus would concentrate on researching statewide (rather than federal) public policy issues, impacting legislation, and lobbying already elected incumbents on certain key pieces of legislation. And they were looking for men and women who could pioneer such efforts in the states.

Susan felt I could fill that bill since I had formerly been a lobbyist for the Building Industry Association in the Palm Springs area and I'd lobbied for the San Bernardino County Council of Real Estate Boards, and I'd lobbied in Sacramento.

*[Susan] suggested that I consider calling Focus and making myself available to them in the worthwhile enterprise proposed in the article.*

I had learned years before that when my bride suggested we consider some course of action, it was truly worth considering. Susan looked at me and simply said, "Call Dr. Dobson."

So I called Dr. Dobson.

Even writing that last sentence makes me laugh. Dr. Dobson and Focus had been such a major player in the raising of our children, in their education, and in so many events in their preteenage years. Susan's offhand suggestion seemed simple enough.

What I did not realize is that, at the time, Dr. James Dobson headed up one of the largest, most well-funded nonprofit organizations in America. Focus's offices were in Pomona, California, and they employed more than nine hundred people at that time. It was kind of a big deal.

But to us, Focus on the Family was just a radio show that helped parents like us raise kids like ours.

The amazing thing was that Dr. Dobson's secretary answered my phone call and responded as if I had been the only one who had ever called his office to talk with him. She graciously told me that he was out of the office but that she'd be honored to introduce me to members of his staff who were involved in the day-to-day operations of public policy. She introduced me to Michael Jameson, who in turn brought me into the circle of other professionals, Steve Knudsen, and John Eldredge. We scheduled time to meet for lunch, and a series of events were set into motion that completely changed the lives of my family. I explained that we'd be moving out of California and if chosen, we'd be honored to serve as lobbyists in other parts of the country. We'd be open to the state of Idaho, if that was a possibility.

John Eldredge was a graduate of my alma mater, Cal Poly, and had done a stint in Washington, D.C., for Gary Bauer of the Family Research Council. He was also an accomplished actor. John took issues very seriously, but he did not take himself seriously.

John's humor struck a chord with me. We found that we had similar tastes, such as Monty Python's classic film *Monty Python and the Holy Grail*—which in time became standard fare for all the Focus on the Family lobbyists and staff members whenever we would meet. We'd repeat lines throughout the flick, laughing as we went. As time rolled on, I introduced the Focus team to *Bill and Ted's Excellent Adventure,* and we began memorizing those lines, too, howling with laughter and enjoying one another's company.

Two years after I arrived in Idaho, I invited John to join us and speak at the first Promise Keepers' meeting held outside of Colorado. I remember John saying that the speakers group of Promise Keepers was a virtual Who's Who, and yet, there he was, a "Who's he?" At the age of eleven, Nate met John and loved listening to his seriousness, humor, and strength—all qualities that Nate appreciated. Nate seemed to love that John Eldredge was a "Who's he?"

John's research and acting ability came together for a key presentation in the '90s—the life of William Wilberforce and his transition from young bon vivant to a serious member of Parliament in the eighteenth and nineteenth centuries, as he worked for the abolition of slavery. John's performance was magnificent. Nate joined John and a dear pilot friend of mine, Harold Thomas, on a whirlwind theater tour of Idaho in which John portrayed Mr. Wilberforce.

Eldredge's star rose further. Years later, in 1999 at an Idaho men's conference called Return to Me, John presented key content that later became the basis for his breakout work *Wild at Heart*. Again, he was simply magnificent in his presentation about searching for one's heart. I was involved in the leadership of the event, and Nate was my right-hand man. Nate enjoyed meeting John again, as well as being challenged regarding where his own wild heart was at age eighteen.

Everything my wife and I touched while joining and working in association with Focus on the Family seemed to flourish, through no natural talent of our own. It was amazingly supernatural.

*Everything my wife and I touched while joining and working in association with Focus on the Family seemed to flourish.*

Dr. Dobson's work seemed to have that very similar supernatural touch.

I discovered differences between Christian activism groups,

which were best represented in a comparison between Dr. Dobson's staff and Pat Robertson's national staff. Where the Focus staff was professionally intense, they also knew how to play. The Christian Coalition folks were always uptight and not very funny.

At the invitation of a friend in national politics, Nancy Bloomer, I attended a private dinner in Boise with a then young Ralph Reed, the executive director of the Christian Coalition and Pat Robertson's right-hand man. I saw absolutely no humor in him, and he never asked me anything about anyone else's family, lives, or interests. He was young and seemed too full of himself. I met him years later, and he had indeed changed, as have we all. Yet, in the '90s, there was a marked difference between the cultures of the key organizations.

At Focus on the Family we simply had fun.

And we tackled the hardest public policy issues of the day: abortion, homosexual rights, choice in education, tax relief, and thousands of state-level pieces of legislation in more than thirty-five state capitols.

Susan and I committed to working with Focus for a decade. We had no idea how that decade would change our family forever. We moved to Idaho and Focus on the Family moved to Colorado Springs, yet our family was what really changed.

First, we *had* to make our annual pilgrimage (our sixth by that time) to Catalina Island and Campus by the Sea. At this critical time of selling our home and our business, the kids wanted something normal, something traditional. The family camp at InterVarsity Christian Fellowship's Campus by the Sea was exactly what we needed. It was a week of joy, normalcy, and learning to live our faith even more deeply. With us going into the ministry, this seemed like something we really had to do. The great thing was that we *all* wanted to go to Catalina.

Susan and I arrived in Boise, Idaho, in August 1991, along with our son, Nate, age ten, and our daughter, Meg, almost seven. Colin was born eight months after we arrived in Idaho. Having left Southern California with high hopes of being accepted by the local Idaho businessmen, elected officials, and ministry leaders, we were not disappointed. Idaho opened its arms to us and allowed us access to the state capitol, to more than 150 churches in the capital city of Boise, and to a list of many businessmen from whom we intended to raise the complete budget for this local lobbying entity that we now called the Idaho Family Forum. Focus on the Family would lend us its name, but it was up to each state family policy council to raise its own budget.

Especially after the joy of Campus by the Sea, Nate did not want to move to Idaho. He fought us tooth and nail the entire time that we were preparing to transition from Southern California to the Pacific Northwest. For a little ten-year-old, he was tremendously persistent. Over and over again we explained that the Lord had opened up the door for us to move to

*Nate's spirit objected and he became disobedient. It was exhausting.*

Idaho; over and over again Nate's spirit objected and he became disobedient. It was exhausting. He was unrelenting. Nate's behavior was classic for a child with ADD, yet we never even considered what he might be dealing with. To us, he was just irritating and selfish. We simply didn't understand him.

It wasn't until he met his new best friend, Mark Smit—who would enter into the world of fourth grade with Nate—that our son smiled. Mark became his friend and brother; the two of them skied together and fully enjoyed Idaho. They laughed till the two sets of parents cried. Paul and Diane Smit were older parents, and

Mark was a miracle baby, arriving after they had adopted his sister, Taryn. Nate, Mark, and their sisters were always a part of the fun when we explored Idaho. Nate's anger with the loss of what he thought he had in California was initially abated to a small degree through his friendship with Mark.

They argued about the funniest things from elementary school through high school. In fact, at Nate's memorial service, Mark spoke humorously about one major debate that followed them into adulthood.

From fourth grade on, Nate and Mark had often debated whether a penny, dropped from the Empire State Building, would, upon impact, have enough force and velocity to injure a person or crack the sidewalk at the base of the building. Pretty scientific, right? Well, sort of.

Apparently, this debate continued for years, and Nate would not let go of it! He argued with Mark at the most inopportune times and in the most unusual places—all the while smirking inside, realizing that he was driving his best friend crazy with this fourth-grade science question. Mark loved Nate's humor and was able to sum up the ongoing decade-plus debate at the memorial service with these simple words: "Nate, you idiot."

Years later, I gained another insight into Nate's fourth-grade self. Bobb Biehl, my good friend and founding board member of Focus on the Family, explained to me that there is a fundamental and significant moment for children at the age of ten (fourth grade) that often defines them for life.

He discovered in his decades of research and in-depth analysis of CEOs that fourth grade was clearly the moment when boys and girls decided without hesitation what they were going to do with their lives, and that intent became the foundation on which the rest of their lives were based. His numbers were staggering. Successful people decided early—in the fourth grade—what they would do and then lived their lives with that key goal in mind.

Nate's rage in the fourth grade in Idaho may have been far more prophetic than we could ever have realized. His friend Mark Smit may have mitigated a portion of the anger, but not much. Nate seemed to channel it into rebellion, even as a preteen. Mark joined him, though his rebellion had limits.

What we had failed to understand was that there would be both an overall *price* and a *cost* for going into the ministry.

## The Price and Cost of Ministry

The *price* of going into the ministry involved lowering our annual income, realizing that we were surrendering what many consider to be life's most productive ten years of earning potential (ages thirty-four to forty-four) so that we could, on many occasions, not receive any income at all. Ministry work is well known for making paupers out of the King's children. We downsized our living arrangements and leased a house, when we were used to buying a home and earning appreciation on its value. Susan and I saw this as just another price of going into the ministry.

*Cost,* on the other hand, is something that has much more profound and long-lasting effects. We easily understand the concept when applied to vehicles or houses: the purchase price is known in both cases; yet the cost of maintaining either of those high-ticket items can be much more than what you have budgeted for.

Applied to our children, the cost of ministry was enormous. The burden came as they watched their dad become either a great champion or an incredibly evil man, depending on who was voicing which opinion.

We started out as anonymous workers in the field of public policy. I simply made myself available to state representatives and senators in the event that they needed research on a particular issue. I remember one legislator's response in particular: "Thank you so much. I never have time to research what I'll soon be voting on. These bills come like water out of a fire hose." My small staff and I researched issues and wrote white papers, so that the legislators would have solid information on which to base their votes.

I remember saying that I wanted ours to be "the most anonymous, well-known work in the state." By that I meant that I wanted to be effective without needing to become well known as an organization or as individuals.

The reality was that as soon as any public policy organization stands against the cultural icons of the day, a target gets affixed to them; sides are picked immediately. Abortion and gay rights have been two of the top issues that have defined political debate in America since the early '70s. As we embraced the discussion and debate of those two issues in

*They watched their dad become either a great champion or an incredibly evil man, depending on who was voicing which opinion.*

the '90s, I became the voice of the religious right in Idaho. Propositions were written that I supported that limited the special rights afforded to homosexuals. I debated these propositions on TV and radio, in print, and via the fledgling Internet. Added to that was the issue of restricting abortion in Idaho. Those two dynamic issues caused a firestorm of anger, disrespect, and division across the

United States, probably rivaled in intensity only by the pre–Civil War debate. Idaho was no different.

In Idaho I became the personification of those issues: for those who opposed special rights for homosexuals and abortion I was their champion—for those who supported those two issues, I stood as the most evil man in the state.

My children were placed in the middle of that confused cacophony of political war cries, with Nate taking the initial brunt of negative comments about his dad. He'd accompany me to church events at which I was the keynote speaker and he'd see well-intentioned Christians fawn over me for my service. In a sense, I became Idaho's James Dobson to many folks. People began to see value in getting information, book leads, or ministry needs to me through my children. Sunday school teachers and other significant adults in my kids' lives treated my son and my daughter indifferently in a class until they discovered the kids' last name—then things became overly friendly and falsely encouraging.

The kids caught on very early. Nate, in particular, hated it. He hated being out at dinner with our family only to be interrupted by some questionably intended sycophant who seemed to feel it was vital that I hear some news on one issue or another. The annoying interruptions were continuous, and Nate hated the often-fanatic display of attention that our family received because of my high-profile job and newly found position in the community.

And that was from friends and supporters.

Opposing the ACLU and the ever-widening collection of sexually charged politics and politically oriented liberal

*Nate hated the often-fanatic display of attention that our family received because of my high-profile job and newly found position in the community.*

individuals was like walking into a barrage of bullets. Some were directed our way through legal opinions against bills we were advancing, others from angry people who simply hated those of us who practiced conventional and orthodox faith.

The 1973 decision on abortion by the U.S. Supreme Court in *Roe v. Wade* had, by the time we began our ministry work in 1990, already allowed more than 20 million babies to be aborted, and there appeared to be no decrease in the number of children who would meet the same fate as the decade of the '90s unveiled itself.

I learned with a legislative bill in the Idaho House and Senate that politics can be a strange thing.

The elections of 1990 were just months away, and the Democrats seized an opportunity to tap into a vein of libertarianism running through Idaho. Using the political and polling advice of David Ripley, the chief political operative for Idaho's arm of the National Education Association, Democrats who had once professed pro-life values committed the Idaho Democratic Party to a new course of defending abortion on demand. Governor Cecil Andrus vetoed the bill. In part because of that divisive abortion battle, which received intense national media attention, Democrats harvested a short-term political gain. They picked up enough seats in the fall to own half the Idaho State Senate. (Their radicalism has, however, cost them dearly in the years since.)

As 1991 opened, the pro-abortion community felt strengthened and ready to push other liberal issues. And into that hot box of political opinion I brought my family. We discussed the different political takes on homosexuality at the dinner table like another family would talk about sports teams. My children saw pictures of aborted babies and knew how many mothers used abortion as a gender-selection technique when they found out they were pregnant. The list of liberal/conservative issues we discussed went on and on.

I remember my seven-year-old daughter at an election event for a mayor, standing at an appetizer table, nibbling. The mayoral candidate came up to her and asked if she had ever been to an event like this. Her answer spoke clearly of how my family and children were familiar with politics. "Oh, yeah," she said, "I go to these things all the time." At that same age, she wrote a short note about the value of babies in their mommies, made fifty copies of the note, and took them door to door on our street. Her note was eventually published as a letter to the editor in the local newspaper.

A bright spot in Nate's life was his love of Boise State University football. When we arrived, two decades ago, the blue turf of BSU football was a new and important sporting feature for locals but had very little play outside the Gem State. Then Head Coach Skip Hall and his wife, Virginia, became friends of our ministry and friends of our family. Nate loved Coach Hall. We attended many of the games, and one year, close to Halloween, Nate asked Coach Hall if he could wear one of the smaller players' orange-and-blue football uniforms. Skip gave him the thumbs-up, and Nate was in football heaven. Nate followed BSU football for the rest of his life. We cherished the photo of twelve-year-old Nate Mansfield in his BSU uniform taking a knee on the blue turf of Boise State University's stadium.

As my kids grew, Nate became more outspoken in public school about key issues. He'd often be the only student in junior high debating the teacher on some intentionally provocative comment about how homosexuals should be allowed to marry. Nate would challenge the teacher and they'd be off to the races. Nate simply did not back down. High school classes brought several more encounters with liberal teachers who knew of Nate's lineage and would intentionally pick verbal fights with him on issues of moral concern. Nate hated being disagreed with by his teachers, yet he knew that he could not let certain things pass as absolute truth when they were only opinions.

At times, I was asked by public school teachers to come speak at some of Nate's classes. I'd ask Nate if he wanted me to attend and would respond accordingly. Initially, more often than not, Nate wanted me to attend. I think he liked how I would debate his teachers on issues.

In time, though, the debate would turn to the topic of legalization of drugs, and a dark cloud would shade Nate's thinking. As time went on, he asked me less and less to attend and debate his teachers. He was gravitating away from us and toward something else—something I did not recognize.

It was often like watching Nate bring fire to his own bosom. The very debate and discussion techniques he had sharpened on issues of moral concern were suddenly being used against my wife and me for the sake of debating the approval of illegal drugs in Idaho and the United States.

The Nate we knew started slipping away.

# Parenting—Are We Done Yet?

There exists in both the Christian community and the secular community an exhausting world of professional parenting.

For the Christian community, it's as if our faith as believers is intimately tied to our sons and daughters—and the value of our very selves, as parents, is tied to the success or failure of how our kids turn out. So we become professionals at parenting—spending copious amounts of time sharpening our skill sets, going to conferences, and reading books whose messages often verge on guilt and condemnation.

The secular community of parenting is not too far behind. With biological clocks ticking, many women over the age of forty who have not yet had a baby are going to extremes to have one. The extremes may involve a wide assortment of techniques, thus producing pregnancy and then, eventually, "the Child" is born.

The bonding bridge between the Christian and secular pursuits of having children may not seem all that clear at first blush. Yet, as you stop and think, the professional parenting emphasis has every-thing to do with producing an offspring so that we as parents can feel complete. It's as if the child will fulfill us in some way that cannot be accomplished in any other way.

And it's exhausting. I know, because I wanted to be the *most* professional parent of them all. And yet, in reality, I needed some-one, somewhere along the way, to tell me, "Dennis, relax. Take a rest."

A selah rest.

"Selah" is the one word used in the book of Psalms to act as a sort of rest for the psalmists or musicians as they present key sec-tions of psalms. You may have seen the word and wondered what it meant.

*The professional parenting emphasis has everything to do with producing an offspring so that we as parents can feel complete.*

But there is so much more to the word.

To the Jewish mind, there was no ques-tion: the word "selah" (*celah* in Hebrew) is an exclamation point of sorts—stating that the reader, the psalmist, the musician should measure and reflect on what has been read or musically performed.

So, I ask you to take a selah rest and reflect on what you've read so far and its application to your life—and the lives of those in your family.

In my life, I never really took that restful time to examine some very key issues. Had I done so, I would have been confronted with some disturbing questions.

For example, I would have had to face the question, "Dennis, are you and Susan child-centered parents?"

Child-centered? What? It's the parenting style that includes our children in everything we do—as if we were trying to gain a level of friendship from our children as one would from adult best friends.

It was as if the exhaustion was an excuse to keep from changing our behaviors. "After all," we rationalized, "we're nearly experts on parenting, and what we've been doing is bringing about marked results and best friends when it's all over."

Yeah, sure. We were teaching our kids to obey on the outside but to sit down in rebellion on the inside. It was as if I wanted my child to be a friend—a really obedient friend who would do as I said. And I'd be much better at it than the next guy.

The world of competitive parenting is tiring. Competing books come out year after year for new parents, and suddenly the newest author is now telling parents that daring to discipline is only half of the equation. The "new" method is strict discipline and the use of a strap on children as old as twelve or thirteen. Then, a backlash erupts and websites go up saying how terrible the strict discipline trainer is. Then, *The world of* a new wave of know-it-alls shows up. *competitive parenting* Now it's all about eating styles. Wait, no, *is tiring.* I mean organic food only and asking the kids what their opinions are on child raising. No, now it's discipline and the 1-2-3s of properly administering this or that. Everyone seems afraid that what they are doing to their children will have an incredibly horrible effect—so they continue their search for the perfect method.

Let me repeat my earlier comment: it is exhausting.

The question is, do we really want to raise children, anyway?

Let me explain.

A clever friend asked me that very question: "Do you really *want* to raise children?"

"Of course I do," I responded, as if my friend were from another planet. "I want to raise *good* children!" I retorted.

He looked at me and simply said, "No you don't."

I was stunned. "Yes I *do* want to raise good children," I told him emphatically.

His response blew me away: "Well, you shouldn't want to raise good children or bad children, for that matter, because you shouldn't want to raise *children* at all!

"You want to raise *adults*, don't you?"

With that one simple question, our terrible world of child-centered, fear-based parenting was turned on its head. We began to take inventory of how we were doing what we were doing. We began to see ourselves as tired and fearful and legalistic and by-the-numbers people. We were parenting by fear, and we were raising children rather than adults.

Nate was quickly becoming the perpetual problem child. Whether it was his early use of marijuana that led to his rebellion or his rebellion that led to his early use of weed and other drugs, both came at us full speed. Before we knew it, we were facing a parent of a high school student who accused Nate of selling weed to his boy. "What are you talking about?" we asked this stranger in our house. "Our son doesn't do drugs," we assured him. And we assured ourselves that we were correct.

Two things began to happen for Nate during this critically important time at the end of high school and thus the end of his time living with us.

Though Nate's world was chaotic throughout high school, we experienced a deep level of joy with our other two children. Key to our change in parenting was the decision to raise adults rather than children—adults who would reap what they sowed and then grow from it. Enabling bad behavior in Nate and his siblings stopped fairly quickly, once we made the choice.

Second, we began to realize that we were taking ourselves far too seriously. Our friend Pastor Tim Remington of Coeur d'Alene,

Idaho, said it this way: "Parenting is overrated."

Pastor Tim's words had a weight and a humor to them that stunned me. Tim's work with evangelical pastors across the United States is well

*Much of what we blame ourselves for . . . could well have popped up in our children's lives regardless of who parented them.*

known. His ministry with our common friend the author Frank Peretti is also well known. When Tim or Frank came to Boise, we were honored to have him stay in our home. Tim has been my good friend for years as well as my mentor for dealing with drug addicts and inmates. His incredible work in the Pacific Northwest is an example for many to follow in the faith-based outreach for healing from drug abuse.

We turned to Tim when the severity of Nate's drug use came to light.

And there he was, telling me, "Parenting is overrated."

He wanted us, I am certain, to realize that much of what we blame ourselves for, as guilt-ridden parents, could well have popped up in our children's lives regardless of who parented them.

And he went on to show us clear biblical examples of parents who were lovers of God, careful and considerate toward their kids, and who, when it all shook out, ended up seeing their own children crash and burn. It was painful to listen to. It was even more painful to read in the Bible.

Most painful was to hear him speak of God's incredible love for His first "son" and the results He was handed, as the consequence of His son's poor choices. It was all flannel-board theology until the name "Adam" was substituted with "Nate."

Tim's experience as a pastor to thousands of ex-addicts became my example of loving people who were unlovable—people who had broken their own families' hearts just as Nate was about to break ours.

Pastor Tim loved our son Nate. He loved Nate's pit bull, Satchel, too. Tim was one of the few strangers who came into Nate's world and wrestled with his "pitty," and Satchel loved it. To Nate, Tim was a real guy and not a religious weirdo.

Tim's words regarding the overemphasis that the Christian community places on parenting began to change our lives.

# Part Two

## A Family in Crisis

# Chapter Eight

# Politics

$P$olitics has both a seductive allure and a repulsive effect. It offers power to those who seek to change the world and a defensive position for those who desire to keep the status quo. Politics has a bright, shiny side—one that was reflected in the vibrant young face of John F. Kennedy during his inaugural and in the more mature words of Ronald Reagan as he stood at the Brandenburg Gate demanding the dismantling of the Berlin Wall.

The most ennobling aspects of politics draw young people to the nation's capital every year with the sincere desire to move along an agenda of hope or tradition or . . . fill in the blank. Youth and politics combine to create new direction for communities both large and small. It can be a very positive force.

Politics also has a dark, ugly side to it.

## Running for Congress

As our decade of working in association with Focus on the Family neared its end, we wanted to finish well. We informed the Idaho Family Forum's board of directors that Susan and I would soon be done with our posts and that we'd be looking at other options as the year 2000 came clearer into focus. Our kids were then eighteen, fifteen, and seven. We sought our children's advice and asked them their thoughts about my possible entrance into elective politics. I was forty-three years old, and after a decade of helping others enter into elective office, it seemed only natural that I would soon follow, first as a candidate and then as an elected official.

But what office?

Running for U.S. Congress seemed like a possibility. Idaho has only two representatives serving in the nation's capital, due to the small population of the state. The incumbent of the district within which I lived was Helen Chenoweth, first elected in 1994 as a supporter of the Contract with America. I'd been a part of her first "kitchen cabinet" as she won the GOP nomination, never thinking that as she honored her pledge to serve only six years that I just might be her successor.

*It seemed only natural that I would soon follow, first as a candidate and then as an elected official.*

My wife supported my desire to run. Nate, in particular, seemed sincerely happy about my opportunity to run and win. He knew how highly visible I was in the community and realized the probability of victory.

Idaho is a Republican state. Once the GOP nomination for a position is secured, that position is often guaranteed in the general election. Hence, the May primary election often holds more drama than the actual election night in November.

So we made the decision to run for U.S. Congress in 2000. Susan and I resigned from ministry in October 1999 and officially announced my candidacy for U.S. Congress in the autumn of that year. We were off to the races and it felt good.

For a season.

The politics of personal intrusion does not only occur in presidential campaigns. The press coverage of the major races is often more visible, but there is also a harsh scrutiny of those who run for U.S. Congress.

Once it was determined that Representative Chenoweth would indeed not run again, the field of candidates grew. Numbering more than a half dozen, the candidates who could raise money and already had a following in the community were reduced to only two: the sitting lieutenant governor of Idaho, Butch Otter, and me. Mr. Otter had an unfair share of negative press due to a recent DUI arrest. I felt for him and never brought up the issue. It was painful enough for his family to have to deal with. And I honestly liked Butch Otter, both then and now.

Yet, as the campaign began to heat up, I looked for chinks in my opponent's armor, seeking help from my son Nate. In high school, Nate had served a number of candidates well, men and women who ran for state legislative races. Every race he helped distribute literature for won! As a sixteen-year-old, Nate helped organize the distribution of literature for a brand-new candidate for the Idaho House of Representatives, Mike Moyle. When the dust settled, the candidate won by thirteen votes—and he attributed much of the reason for the win to Nate's tireless work. As of this book's writing, that elected official is now the GOP majority leader for the House of Representative in Idaho. Nate ran the campaign literature distribution for other candidates and was paid well for his service. He loved working for Shirley McKague, a capitol secretary who ran first for State House. Nate helped her win! She recently retired from the Idaho Senate.

So it only seemed natural that I should ask Nate for help in my own race for U.S. Congress. Lieutenant Governor Otter had recently run afoul of the Environmental Protection Agency, and the press was all over him. As a wealthy man, Otter owned a substantial amount of land. In a portion of that land, he had a pond. It was his land. It was his pond. Yet he was "caught" draining it and was fined by the EPA for tampering with a wetlands area.

At the time, Nate told me that it was not an issue worth pursuing, but an out-of-area consultant in the campaign felt it was. I chose the consultant's advice over my son's and made a mountain out of a molehill. In Idaho, the EPA is no one's friend. Doing what Butch did made him a bit of a hero to many folks. My insistence on making it a campaign issue was foolishness. And it was wrong. It had no traction with the voters and made me look small in my criticism of the lieutenant governor.

*My insistence on making it a campaign issue was foolishness. And it was wrong.*

Nate knew his stuff.

The autumn turned into the end of the year, and the congressional campaign continued. A great campaign manager was chosen: Christy Oetken. My race in Idaho was selected as the first primary race for a newly formed group called the Committee for Growth—a Washington, D.C., political action committee formed by supporters of the Cato Institute. Hundreds of thousands of independent dollars began flowing into the race. Relationships that I had formed throughout my decade of working in association with Dr. Dobson's group began to flower and produce fruit. It was as if the movement we needed was being delivered up at exactly the right and proper time.

With one small problem.

## *Trouble with Nate*

Nate's attitude began to sour. He became belligerent and defensive. His circle of friends had changed so much that we only knew three or four of them. His best friend since childhood, Mark Smit, seemed to be replaced by people we didn't know and who did not care to know us. He began his senior year in high school just after his eighteenth birthday, so he felt he was an adult. Rules became meaningless and curfews were a joke. He came and went as if he were a boarder and we were nothing more than landlords. We were busy with the race for Congress, and he eventually became distant and then invisible.

By mid-January of his senior year, Nate's behavior was beyond surly. Finally, we'd had enough. Taking a break from the campaign, I asked him to sit with us so we could redefine our relationship. His response was explosive—utterly without any precedent. He cursed me, walked into his room, and threw clothes into a sports bag, screaming at his mom and me. It was a scene of insanity. My anger level was sky high. I could usually take his occasional outbursts and his ongoing foulmouthed foolishness when it was directed at me. But when he began berating his mother, I was finished with him.

Sensing that he had gone too far, Nate met me in the entrance of our house with his sports bag full of clothes. Chest to chest, he looked me in the eye and screamed into my face, "I am out of here.

I will see you in the obituaries." He swiveled and was through the door in seconds. He walked over to my car in the driveway and spit on its windshield.

Our son was gone.

My wife was in tears. She ran into another room with me in pursuit. She was sobbing and couldn't believe that this was how our son was leaving our house in the middle of his senior year—with threats and yelling, with dishonor and anger. I held Susan in my arms as she sobbed and sobbed. My own tears were of anger and the deepest of sadness. Our sobs blended as we wondered what had just happened. We would find out later—at a huge cost—why this January outburst had occurred.

It's hard to pursue goals—especially those involving family—when your own family is disintegrating right before your eyes. Running for U.S. Congress became enormously difficult. I found very little help from key men whom I had mentored during my ministry days. One in particular berated me, believing that Nate's behavior was directly proportionate to my failure as a father. Another simply laughed off the tough times we were facing with Nate, saying it was "regular teenage drama." I was deeply disappointed by the second man years later when he failed to come to Nate's funeral. In some small way, though, I could understand. I too had once been a person who knew all the answers about child rearing—or at least believed I did.

The race for Congress took on a life of its own. The pressure to raise money, to be present at events, to be clever and witty, and to navigate the teeming waters of political infighting within the Republican Party ratcheted up the tension.

Nate's absence was like a perpetual migraine, one that never left and from which I could receive no relief. He was living at his friend's house, sleeping on the couch, finishing his senior year. He didn't call us; he despised us. His friend's parents seemed to believe his story—that I was too strict and gave him no freedom—over and over again.

At some point, Nate began losing sight of others, including

*It's hard to pursue goals—especially those involving family—when your own family is disintegrating right before your eyes.*

the people with whom he was staying. The same cycle of behavior began—late nights, doing what he wanted, using drugs, being belligerent and defensive—this time with them. It took only three months for the other family to realize what we had had to deal with for several years. Nate was too independent an individual to act any other way.

The only problem with that type of selfish, angry behavior is that people who don't love you won't put up with you.

His friend's parents asked him to leave and suggested he make up with his parents and his family.

With their assistance, he realized that the only option for safe living was moving back to Mom and Dad's house—ninety days after having thrown down the gauntlet of independence.

What at first seemed to be a version of the prodigal son later revealed itself to simply be a need for three hots and a cot. Apologies preceded the request, but it wasn't clear whether our son had any idea how much his previous behavior had pained his parents. My guess is that he didn't care. He needed free room and board and knew his family would take him back in until he graduated and moved on to college. We heard his words, saw his apparent honesty, and opened our door to him. We saw his conniving, too. We simply chose to overlook it, due to our hurting hearts.

Nate settled back into his old room. It was an uneasy truce. It was a do over, and we'd wait and see how well he'd do.

Amid that entire chaotic episode, I kept running for Congress, believing that a May victory was right around the corner. I wondered what it would be like to spend my upcoming summer vacation at Campus by the Sea as a nominee to the U.S. House of Representatives—with my family and my newly returned son by my side. I was envisioning a fairy tale, a false reality.

*What I failed to understand was that there had been a reason for Nate's incredible anger in January.*

What I failed to understand was that there had been a reason for Nate's incredible anger in January.

Nate had committed a crime at the first of the year that would impact us for the rest of our lives—and he knew it. No wonder he was furious—at himself.

*Chapter Nine*

# The Dark World of Loss

$G$ood elections are like good motion pictures. The story line unfolds, the characters come into focus at key moments along the way, and sidebar stories are introduced. Long, intense moments of dialogue lull the viewer into a mood of quietness, and then suddenly—at an unexpected interval—the climactic moment of the film occurs with its surprising outcome, followed shortly by a brief scene or two summing up the entire film.

In presidential campaigns, the storylines are bigger than life and the characters take on a status far greater than they should: Did this candidate finish college? Did that candidate's wife have a previous marriage that went bad? Is there a failed business in his background? On and on the sidebar questions stretch.

When the political election is for U.S. Congress, the intensity of the questions and probing is not as severe—not what Hollywood would have you believe.

U.S. Congressional races do, indeed, touch on national issues, but the races are simply regional. A local newspaper journalist interviews the candidate in between doing stories about a cancer victim's Race for the Cure or a fire that swept through a city's industrial area. A candidate running for U.S. Congress is not big news.

That is, unless a controversial story breaks right before Election Day.

And by the way, the controversial story must have a "man bites dog" angle to it, so that the electorate doesn't believe it's just more mudslinging by one candidate against another. Voters have grown indifferent to orchestrated election attacks. Unplanned-for chaos, however, is a completely different story. It's a form of acceptable gossip that voters have grown to expect—and they enjoy it.

Our preelection polling showed that our campaign was within 3 to 5 percentage points of victory—thus, a statistical dead heat. It was an amazing feat, given that the lieutenant governor's successful election record showed a string of victories over several decades. I'd never run for an office in Idaho and was known chiefly for being the Focus on the Family guy. Mr. Otter must have seen similar polling numbers and responded with immediate action, advancing more than $150,000 of his personal funds to his campaign to buy last-minute media time. He seemed scared.

Five days before the primary election for U.S. Congress, my opponent and I had a television debate. The lieutenant governor, the other candidates, and I squared off with one another; the issues of the day were debated clearly, showing the differences of perspective among all of us. It was a fun exercise and appeared to help the viewers who wanted to make an intelligent decision.

## A Shocking Revelation

As the debate ended and handshakes were exchanged among all the opponents and their staffs, a reporter approached me as I stepped down from the podium. "Mr. Mansfield, I'm so-and-so from such-and-such newspaper. Is your oldest son's name Nathan Dennis Mansfield?"

I stood frozen for a second.

I'd been interviewed enough times over the past ten years so that I can quickly assess the direction in which a reporter wants to take an interview. The debate that night had me firing on all cylinders—I was ready for anything.

Except for this simple, factual question about my son's three names. I knew in an instant that something really bad had happened. A question by a reporter referencing the full three legal names of any person is not a good thing.

*I knew in an instant that something really bad had happened.*

"Yes it is," I responded. "Why?"

"Well, sir, were you aware that Nathan was arrested this past January on a drug paraphernalia charge?"

I stood speechless. I probably looked stunned. My mind immediately searched for anything that would help me get a fix on what had happened, when it had happened, and why it had happened.

January? That was the month Nate blew up and moved out.

"Mr. Mansfield, excuse me. Were you aware?" he asked almost impatiently.

"No, I was not aware," I answered curtly. "But I will meet with my son tonight and find out what this is all about."

As I exited the television studio, I got on my cell phone and reached out to my father, Bill Mansfield, and my friend Michael Boerner. I asked both men to meet with Nate and find out exactly what had happened and to do it ASAP. I was too furious with Nate to meet with him myself. I needed time to think and process. The political fuse was burning down to the explosion. The reporter was from a weekly paper, and his print deadline was the next day, giving us forty-eight hours before the story blew up on the streets. Because there was little online presence yet, we had a slight window of opportunity to figure out what to do. It was our plan to use that window to react correctly and honestly as a congressional campaign.

But we were more than a campaign in crisis. We were a family in crisis. My son had been arrested? *My son?* When? How? Why? The questions engulfed my wife and me.

My father and my friend quickly found Nate, met with him, and determined the nature and time frame of the arrest.

I now realized that I needed to wrestle with the simple reality that my son had committed an illegal act, had been arrested, and that all we had raised him to be now seemed cast aside. I struggled with the picture of him in jail, around druggies and convicts. My son. My beautiful Nate. And I knew *nothing* about it.

And then I realized, *I need to see Nate and hear his story. I need to go to my son.*

## Nate's Confession

I shot across town and met the three men at our campaign headquarters. I walked into the conference room. Nate stood up. I walked directly over to him and hugged him with all that was inside of me.

"Nate, I love you," I told him. We began crying.

The four of us sat down; the men closest to me told me the details of Nate's arrest five months before. He had been

*We had to deal with the political fallout of the Focus on the Family guy losing all control of his family.*

arrested in a park with a friend of his, sitting in a car. Inside the car was a pipe for smoking crack and black tar heroin. Nate's charge was possession of drug paraphernalia. And he was guilty. He was also deeply regretful and fully repentant and asked for our forgiveness, through his tears.

He admitted it all to me, to his grandfather, and to our family friend Michael Boerner. We forgave him. Because we loved him, the personal side could heal quickly.

The public side would have a life all its own.

We had to deal with the political fallout of the Focus on the Family guy losing all control of his family—at least in the eyes of the voters, who would be choosing their next U.S. congressman in just five days.

My mind immediately ran to the political side of the issue and subsequent questions: "Why had this taken five months to surface?" and "How was it that the court case was listed just one week before the primary election?" To this day, I am certain that, as in any community, there were people who used the court system's calendar to manipulate our family's tragedy for someone else's benefit. It was unconscionable, and yet it was real.

Nate asked if he could call a press conference to announce what was about to break in the newspaper. My father and our friend felt that Nate's years of being involved in political races and in the media, coupled with his sincere repentance for what he'd done, made a press conference in the morning an immediate priority.

Nate's hair was a mop. He looked horrible, like a druggie. Someone suggested we find a barber, which Nate agreed to, but by this time it was almost midnight. Our campaign manager, Christy Oetken, knew how to cut hair, so we decided to let her resurrect her clipper skills. Within minutes, my son looked like the old Nate—clean-cut and wide awake. He was even smiling, knowing that a weight he had carried for five months was now off his back. Our problem was, it was now in the public for everyone to weigh in on.

## The Whirlwind Before the Fall

The next series of events blended together like an Impressionist painting. The following morning's press conference was held in our home. We limited attendance and angered many people in the media—not inviting many reporters who had never shown even the slightest kindness to my family or to me. Papers, TV, radio, and the fledgling Internet were ablaze with the story of the day, certainly of the week, maybe of the election cycle. Terrible pieces were written about me, calling me names and suggesting that I tortured my son with my religious beliefs and my hypocrisy. It was horrible to live through for our entire family. People flooded talk radio shows to give their expert opinions on the smallest parts of the story. I became a monster, and Nate became a drug addict in the minds of many voters and others. It was the longest five days of our family's life. Election Day arrived, like an unwelcomed veterinarian showing up to put down a sick family dog.

The Election Day's results were dismal. In a field of six or eight candidates, I came in a distant second to the lieutenant governor, losing by almost twenty-two points. News of the story of

Nate's arrest breaking so close to the primary was damaging and had thrown my campaign's closing fight for undecided voters into instant disarray.

As is the custom with candidates on election night, I held a "victory party" at our headquarters, inviting hundreds of volunteers to come and participate. The mood was low. Nate showed up. I met him outside the campaign headquarters and stood next to him. He was sobbing uncontrollably. "You lost because of me," he said repeatedly. I could not comfort him or assuage the guilt of his conclusion. There was no way for me to pretend that the loss wasn't in part due to his behavior and arrest. Instead, I simply held him in my arms. Even though Nate's arrest had alienated some voters, contrary to his guilty statement, almost never does a win or loss come down to a single factor.

Nate was distraught because of what he'd done, and though I was deeply saddened because I'd lost an opportunity for a seat in the U.S. Congress, what I really didn't want to lose was my son.

But that was not within my control.

Guilt manifests itself in many ways. For some, the experience of being arrested, having a public display of the arrest, contributing to an election loss in such a grand way, and then falling contritely at your father's feet would be enough to amend illegal behavior. For many people, but not for Nate.

## Old Patterns Reemerge

From the time he was little, Nate had evidenced patterns verging on obsessive-compulsive behavior. As a young boy, he'd scour the convenience stores for soft drink bottles that had contest tabs hidden inside the cap. He'd either buy as many as he could or he'd tip the bottle so he could discern whether that particular bottle cap was a winner. He would not give up. Baseball cards became an addiction in his youth. He had thousands of cards and learned everything he could about each team and each player, focusing in on Ken Griffey, Jr., of course.

Never, during those many years of quirky behavior, did we think that illegal and prescription drugs would become the ultimate object of his obsession. Soon after the high-profile public exposure of Nate's drug use, he was arrested in an adjoining county for possession of materials to "huff." Huffing is the inhaling of certain spray chemicals that create a high. He and my wife went to the initial court hearing to receive the charges.

I will never forget Nate's reaction when he and Susan entered the house after going to court. Smiling and almost giddy, Nate shouted as he walked in the door, "Wow, Dad, you really pulled some strings on *that* one. The policeman never even showed up in court, so the case was thrown out. That's so cool how you got to the cop and made him do that!"

*I will never forget Nate's reaction when he and Susan entered the house after going to court.*

I was stunned. I stood there and looked at him in the entrance of our house and said, as I violently shook my head, "I never called the deputy sheriff who arrested you. I'd never, ever do that, Nate." But Nate wouldn't believe me. He left the house crowing about how I had helped get him off. I was losing my son to drugs and to the culture that supports and encourages it; I could see it in his face and hear it in his deceived voice.

Later, I looked up the name of the deputy sheriff who made the arrest and called him to find out what had happened. My wife and

I wanted Nate to feel the full impact of what was slowly but surely becoming his way of life. The deputy told me that he was called away on another case on that particular court date and, "besides, Nate's your son, and I know that you're thought highly of in the community for your strong stand on families, so I figured he'd catch hell from you. Incarceration for a young man just on minor charges doesn't help anyone." This well-meaning deputy sheriff did us no favors.

Nate's minor arrests continued; as an adult he was no longer living with us, and we were no longer aware of his arrests. Even today, I simply do not know how many times Nate Mansfield was arrested. Misdemeanors have little impact on people who have been arrested for significant offenses. Judges often attempt to keep certain behavioral types out of the mainstream of felony convicts. Wisely, these judges have decided that they do not want young impressionable men and women to become career criminals by moving them up to felony status.

But some people simply do not learn. Or they truly believe that the law applies to everyone except them. I sense that Nate fell into this second category. He knew who he was in Christ and that whatever he was doing was only "temporary" in its consequences, so he thought he could do as he pleased. He felt he always had special sanctions and thus the bad things that happened to other people would not happen to him.

He distanced himself from us and moved around—and we often lost track of him. While living in Oregon, he decided to travel with some high school friends to a rock concert in Tennessee. We were never informed and didn't hear about the trip until things went bad. Leaving the concert and beginning the long drive back to Idaho, Nate and his friends were pulled over in the northeast corner of Missouri; their 1969 VW bus had a taillight out. The local police found scales, plastic bags, and evidence of THC (a chemical in marijuana that can be sprayed on legal tobacco to attain the high of marijuana). All four young men were arrested and placed in Montgomery County Jail in Missouri.

The minor problems had just turned into major ones. The parents of the other three young men hired attorneys and bailed them out of jail so they could return home to Idaho and begin making their defense for the court hearing. We decided to let Nate sit in jail. He was furious with us. It seemed to us that he needed to serve some time. "Tough love" many people call it; all we knew was that he'd been given so many chances and now he was at a judge's mercy.

Nate stayed in jail for several weeks and ultimately stood before a judge who saw my son's value. The sentence was Solomon-like: Nate and his friends were given five-year felony convictions that would reduce if they finished their college degrees within four years. The judge released them with these words: "You are good kids. You're better than this. Go get your education and leave this episode behind you." His friends flew home, but Nate returned to our hometown by bus. The trip took several days, but he did not care. He was free and he was happy.

Upon Nate's return to Idaho, we took him to breakfast and saw what appeared to be a genuine change of behavior. He was clean and sober, he was free, and he wanted to start over. He was our son, smiling and hopeful.

*He was clean and sober, he was free, and he wanted to start over.*

Yet in too short a period of time, Nate sought out his old group of friends, and the roller coaster of bad behaviors began again. His return to college at Boise State University proved to

A band of brothers and sisters. Back row: Kathy, Dennis, Gary. Front row: Janet, Joyce, JoAnne, and Ken. *(Photograph © Bill Mansfield)*

Regaining our joy. Susan and Colin as he finished West Point's Beast Barracks in 2010. *(Family photograph)*

Campus by the Sea today— missing Nate and yet feeling his presence. *(Family photograph)*

LEFT: Colin at West Point, class of 2014. *(Photograph © Kyle Morgan)*

RIGHT: Nate always supported Colin's Boy Scout years. He also loved West Point. *(Photograph © Troy Maben)*

LEFT: The infectious joy of a clean and sober Nate Mansfield. *(Family photograph)*

RIGHT: Bill Mansfield and his granddaughter Meg. *(Family photograph)*

Captured by the fumes of high school: car fumes and perfumes. *(Family photograph)*

We learned to be content, joyous, and even happy, despite the depth of pain that came our way. *(Photograph © Marcee Roberts)*

A member of the West Point class of '78, plebe year (1975). *(Family photograph)*

A young family—loving the newness of it all. *(Photograph © Henri Raynaud)*

Nathan the Adventurer. *(Photograph © Henri Raynaud)*

The ladies of our house—Susan and Megan. *(Photograph © Henri Raynaud)*

A family reunited—
Nate's release
from prison, 2005.
*(Photograph © Leo Geiss)*

Campaign 2000. Nate would come
out from the background in ways
I never expected. *(Photograph © Stan
Sinclair)*

The 2000 race for U.S.
Congress—a family under
siege. *(Photograph © Stan
Sinclair)*

Nate loved our family—his family—with all his heart.
*(Family photograph)*

My daughter, Meg, on her wedding day.
*(Family photograph)*

Nate's teasing was evident even during photo sessions. Meg took it in stride. *(Photograph © Stan Sinclair)*

Nate and Ginny, getting ready to start their future together.
*(Photograph © Angie Ross)*

Taking a knee on Boise State's blue turf. Even as a ten-year-old, Nate rooted for the underdog. He loved BSU when the nation hadn't noticed them. *(Family photograph)*

The men of the house—Colin, Nate, and Den. *(Photograph © Troy Maben)*

Before babies. Newly married and looking on a bright future. *(Family photograph)*

Nate and his fiancée, Ginny.
*(Family photograph)*

The congressional
candidate's wife.
*(Family photograph)*

The last picture we have with
Nate on Catalina Island, 2000.
*(Family photograph)*

This snapshot, right around Nate's
twenty-first birthday, shows our
mutual love, respect, and fun. *(Family
photograph)*

be a farce; he simply dismissed the chance that the Missouri judge gave him by saying, "I'll just never go back to Missouri; then they can't arrest me." Our hearts were broken, again. His friends' philosophy became his philosophy; his loyalty to drug addicts became the definer of his future.

In time, Nate became addicted to oxycodone, an opium-based drug made famous by the arrest and rehab of Rush Limbaugh. Nate met a network of older people who were ill with cancer and other diseases and had legal prescriptions and who would sell excess pills to prescription drug addicts like my son. The underground network proved to be extensive; it was primarily made up of retired people who needed money and found willing recipients for additional prescriptions. In Nate's case, the pills were sold to him for forty or fifty dollars each. To an addict working a typical forty-hour job, the price of these pills was manageable. But when either the addiction level increased or the employment hours decreased, the ability to purchase the pills would dry up and another drug would have to be found.

The normal substitute for unemployed and broke addicts is heroin.

It is cheap and available, and it became the drug of choice for our son. Our beautiful Nate was now a heroin addict.

In time, that addiction became all consuming, eventually forcing his probation officer to arrest Nate for violating the Missouri probation agreement. He was also charged for a new violation: possession and use of black tar heroin. Nate was sentenced to a year in our local county jail. Our sadness and sense of loss deepened exponentially. How could broken people be even more smashed to pieces? How could our son—who year after year had gone to Christian school and Campus by the Sea, and who had traveled on foreign missions all across the world—end up in a cell with the moral and legal reprobates of our city? The harder question was, how was it that Nate was a reprobate?

## The Walking Dead

We no longer had answers. We were spiritually drained parents for whom nothing worked—nothing from Christian bookstores or Sunday school lessons or Christian radio programs or Promise Keepers or Focus on the Family or . . .

We were the walking dead, and dead people eventually become odorous to friends and family. Our aloneness and loneliness intersected in the absence of understanding by fellow believers. We were outsiders on the inside of the body of Christ. Like lepers we were treated as unclean by scared Christian parents who were fearful that their own children would become like our son. After all, if it could happen to the Focus on the Family parents, it could also happen to the young couples that had formerly looked up to us.

> *We were the walking dead, and dead people eventually become odorous to friends and family.*

The only place, as a couple, we could focus our energies was toward our son in jail. We visited him often, and we developed a regular letter-writing campaign. Nate reciprocated the letters, and through the medium of the written word, we began to read how he felt and thought. We sent books for him to read, and he devoured them like a starving man devours food. Close friends and family joined us in sending more books. It was remarkable to see his vocabulary expand due to his reading and being clean from drugs. It was as if the major authors of our time became his personal tutors.

Much of the drug-related chaos in our family subsided while Nate was in our local jail. We met with him and spoke on phones through thick glass panels about life and God. We accepted pay phone calls from him. As Nate's year moved through the four seasons, none of his drug friends visited him. Not a single one. Not even his best friend, not the young man whose house he lived in during his senior year. No one visited Nate in jail other than his family and two pastors he didn't know—one in particular, David Snyder, visited him regularly. Nate was left alone and uncared for, because those who use drugs care only for themselves. In time, Nate saw himself in them and admitted that they really didn't care deeply about what he was facing, just as he had not cared for us when he was high. A bitterness brewed in Nate against these men and women.

I wrote him a very strong letter during this time period.

*December 1st, 2004*

*Dear Nate,*

*It was nice talking to you on the jail payphone. Thanks for calling.*

*I received your letter from jail, written the day before Thanksgiving. I was thankful that you wrote it and glad that you expressed yourself. I acknowledge your positions and want you to know that the letter did not hurt me. You've written from your pain and that helps both of us. Thanks for being open.*

*In years past I would have harshly reacted to your letter rather than patiently responding. In doing so, I most assuredly would have hurt you. Not this time around, though. I've learned a lot this past year. I've learned that it is not healthy to try and talk a person out of how they feel about a subject. Somehow the message and the method both hurt.*

Through a friend, I once heard this phrase: "Truth never fears investigation." I'd add to that phrase: "neither does pain fear investigation." So let's investigate a few things in this letter, knowing that the backdrop of it is this: I will not try to change your worldview and that I deeply love you.

Sound like a deal? Okay, let's dive in, remembering that all ideas have consequences.

You made some very good and truthful arguments in your letter about being burned out on thinking that God will help you. You acknowledge that what you've got facing you is what you did to yourself. Okay, that's true. No need to investigate it. It is plain for each of us to see. I also agree that no Christian books are going to change your mind. You're not there. Your spirit is not there. If your spirit were there, you would want to read those things. Simple logic dictates that. Again, we both agree. You simply behave as though you do not need God. Your belief system is translated out by your behavior system.

*I've learned a lot this past year. I've learned that it is not healthy to try and talk a person out of how they feel about a subject.*

You also don't want to go through rehab. No problem. Those people who wanted to help you believed that you wanted to help yourself. You don't want to help yourself move away from drugs. So, it would be deceitful to take their funds and apply the money to something that you just won't do, or that you would con folks, if you were to attend. Okay, we will send those funds back to them and we will not pursue a reservation at rehab unless something changes.

Next, the funds from the sale of your truck need to go

*somewhere. When we understood that you wanted to change positions on the use of illegal drugs, we were ready to apply them to the rehab. As you do not wish to embrace this type of plan, we will use the funds to pay back family members (us) and others to whom you owe debt.*

*Regarding your precious dog, Satchel, I'd say that you were pretty darn fortunate to have your sister and brother-in-law agree to a year-long commitment to watch your dog. They are six months into it, and it appears that you and they will have to figure out if he stays with them past the one-year mark. Maybe yes, maybe no. They have their own life to lead and it originally did not have plans for your dog.*

*Since you are not going to rehab and have therefore ruled out even the possibility of Satchel going with you to a rehab center (but would rather face prison time), something eventually needs to be done with Satchel. Your actions will prompt the next event(s) in your dog's life. Those decisions, however, are solely Meg and Caleb's and not Mom's and mine. We will support them.*

*You love Satchel and that is clear. He has been one of your biggest successes in life. And he is a fine success. We have all fallen in love with your dog. But in a sense you have not loved him as much as Meg has proven that she loves Satchel. Let me explain: Had you indeed loved your dog with ALL that you are, you would never have endangered him by putting him in this current position. He can't stay where he is forever. Because you are living as a drug addict, your dog faces the fate of a drug addict's dog. I believe they will choose wisely, though. And by the way, how you feel right at this moment, regarding Satchel not being in your life and potentially being at risk, is how Mom and I feel about you, only one hundred times stronger a feeling for us.*

*You mention that you could do prison time "standing on your head." Brave words from someone in a county jail who has not been to prison. I know men who have been there. You have no idea what you are facing, Nate. You have no "truth" on this issue. You have adolescent fantasy thoughts linking Tony Montana to Blow's George, but you don't know . . . and won't know until the day you enter prison, should that occur. How sad a day that would be for you and us.*

*The equally sad thing is that we, as human beings, don't NEED to experience painful things to know that they hurt. It appears that you feel you have no other option but to feel these painful things. I think you are wrong, and way too cavalier in your approach to life-changing, life-staining places and events.*

*The truth is, that you could be doing EVERYTHING in your power to NOT go there. But you have resigned yourself to such a future and you have designed for yourself such a future. You are choosing to do this. And I believe it will prove to be painfully foolish.*

*This is reality, Nate, not TV or the movies. So where can you gain "hope" in this hopeless situation?*

*Here is another shocker for you: You can't. Not living as you have lived. True hope can only come from the Lord. Not from friends, not from family, not from judges. Hope comes from God. So does mercy.*

*So this brings us around to the topic of God's nature. You have stated that you believe He is a passive, uninvolved God who started things and walked away. Call yourself, then, a deist, but cease referring to yourself as a Christian. Truthfully, a Christian is a believer in Jesus, the personal Savior for individuals.*

*To believe in Jesus the Messiah is to believe this: that He exists, that He took on your "sentence to eternal Hell"* rather than make you serve it, and that He is involved in the daily affairs of man. He does this through the power of the Holy Spirit, whom He left on Earth as the "comforter" to mankind, one personal spirit at a time. (That's part of the definition of the Trinity.) He is definitely involved, not a type of grandfather at all.*

*If you had treated a friend with the distance and disinterest that you treated the Lord— would that friend still be around?*

*It just doesn't seem that way to you right now because you chose to break off your relationship with Him, rather than the other way around. Think if you had treated a friend with the distance and disinterest that you treated the Lord—would that friend still be around? Or would he be at the distance you placed him, waiting to be asked back into your life?*

*The gentle grandfather thing doesn't mesh well with the wild-eyed, white-haired return of a fiery Jesus as God in The Book of the Revelation, who will allow two-thirds of mankind to send themselves to Hell. So, be truthful with yourself. If you disagree with what Mom and I, Meg, Colin, Caleb, Corey, Gabe, Mrs. Oster, the Smits, Grand Pa and Grandma Mansfield, my sisters and brothers, Grandma, Larry, Julie, Andrew, and so many others in your "life quilt" believe about the nature and character of God, then embrace it. But remember: two direct opposite positions cannot both be true . . . and truth never fears investigation.*

*But, Nate, if you DO believe that Jesus is who He says He*

*is and if you DO believe in traditional orthodoxy . . . not in deism, then my next question is this: Why are you fighting against what you believe?*

*If I said I loved Mom and yet cheated on her throughout the twenty-seven years of our marriage, you would rightly question the validity of my beliefs. Saying something doesn't make it so. Not in marriage and not in life. Living it makes it so.*

*That's why in the Bible, James said that faith without works is dead. I may be wrong, but it appears your life is one of works without faith . . . and your works have gotten you where you are today . . . in jail and possibly bound for prison.*

*So, how's that working for you, Nate? No wonder you are low and sad. No wonder you are depressed. You appear to be living a life directly opposite to what you truly know and believe to be true (and were raised to live). You seem to be lying to yourself, and your spirit has been twisted painfully out of shape for years and years. Is that so? Only your spirit knows, Nate. But I sense it is true. Investigate it and see, because Truth never fears . . .*

*I love you,*
*Dad*

## Pastor Snyder

Pastor David Snyder decided to invest regularly in our son. Pastor Dave had never even met Nate before. Nor would he ever see him outside of the thick-glassed walls of pastoral visiting rooms at the county jail.

Here is how Pastor Dave put it:

*Nate and I met for the first time in jail. He was an inmate and I was a visitor. This particular institution didn't allow face-to-face visits. Between the glass and phone booth handsets—that was it.*

*It was the only way I ever knew Nate.*

*His parents were my friends and, through them, I'd learned of Nate's addiction and ensuing incarceration. Nate, though, was a piece of their lives with which I had no experience. When his choices and God's specialized plan of formation landed him in the local jail, I went to see him. Largely, I wanted to bless his parents, Dennis and Susan. And, I hoped to speak life to Nate. God allowed me to do both.*

Pastor David Snyder's impact on Nate and his review of Nate's theological point of view was so vital to understanding how our son moved from an award-winning Awana Bible Quiz student to an incarcerated heroin addict that I've place his perspective as a complete chapter, later on in this book.

So, on a cold February day, at the 365-day mark, Nate finished his sentence in the local Idaho jail and was swept away to Missouri by an interstate extradition service. It seemed the wise Missouri judge wanted to see Nate. Where jail was excruciating for all of us, it became exceedingly clear that our son was now headed to a deeper, darker life.

He would soon be two thousand miles away from his family.

Not just in a local jail, but in a Missouri state prison.

# Chapter Ten

# Incarceration

The lyrics of John Lennon's song "Beautiful Boy" were prophetic in many ways. "Life is what happens to you while you're busy making other plans . . ."

Our years' worth of making "other plans" for entrance into the U.S. Congress had blown up in our faces; not unlike so many families who face the agonizing and unexpected interruptions of their lives by sons and daughters who are sidetracked by drugs, mental illness, and victimization. We honestly did not know where to turn.

## *Faced with Failure*

After so many years of directing parents as to how they should raise their children, I looked the hypocrite and possibly was one on many levels. Susan and I had believed that child raising involved a methodical step-by-step process. And we believed that if you followed these steps, you were guaranteed success. But that's not how things turned out. We now found ourselves with no method that worked and no process that had been successful with our oldest child.

Chief to our dismay was the fact that Nate was our *oldest* child. A little over three years separate him from our second child and almost eleven years from our third, so for all we knew the next two kids were on a similar path that would duplicate many of the problems we currently faced.

Trailblazing with such a disruptive first child creates no real pathways except those of fear and negative reactions. Facing his incarceration in a state prison facility was more than our hearts could take. Like so many moviegoers, we'd seen documentary and feature films that portrayed the violence, sexual abuse, and depravity of prison. The atrocities these movies portrayed would soon be a part of our son's life—day in and day out.

> *While our son was in jail (now prison), we knew he was alive and we knew he was being fed and clothed.*

I remember a phone call Nate and I shared once he arrived at his in-processing prison in Missouri. While I was advising Nate about situations to avoid, he stopped me and simply said, "Dad, I am a man. I got myself in here, and I can protect myself while I am here." He said this with a tired, confident voice. I realized how much he had matured, as a result of his own pain.

We did know this: while our son was in jail (now prison), we knew he was alive and we knew he was being fed and clothed. For much of his independent life as a drug user, there were many days and even weeks where we were not sure of his well-being.

Strangely, we somehow knew he'd be safe in prison, especially in light of his initial comments to me before his in-processing.

# *Difficult Decisions*

Susan and I decided *not* to go to Missouri to plead Nate's case before the judge who had originally sentenced him. There was no need to. Nate was guilty. He had already had his second chance. We struggled with how this would look to Nate—as if we, too, had abandoned him at his moment of sentencing, as had his high school and college friends. Having had the assurance that, as a man, he was willing to take what the system was going to give him, we chose to visit him only when he was released.

When it came time for his sentencing, Nate made a cross-country van/bus trip in handcuffs and prison garb and stood before the same Missouri judge as before. The sentence was harsh, deliberate, and without mercy. Nate would receive a felony conviction (now his second or third; we simply did not know). He would never be able to vote again, he could never serve either in the military or as an elected official, he could never own a weapon, and he would serve no less than two years in prison, with time allotted for what he had served in the local Idaho county jail. When his time was served, he would be on parole for seven years, and anytime his parole officer felt Nate was injurious to the community, our son would be returned to prison to serve the rest of his sentence. Nate was facing the next decade of his life behind bars if he continued with his rebellious ways.

This was the fruit borne from Nate Mansfield's life.

When Nate told us the verdict over the phone, we were sickened. The long-term effect was disastrous to Nate, and he didn't even seem to care. "With time served, I'll be out of prison within a year," he boasted. A year . . . another year. From the time he was twenty years old to the time he turned twenty-five, Nate would spend four of his actual birthdays behind bars. "I can do this time standing on my head," he carelessly blurted out to me. I remember sobbing on the phone and then suddenly stopping when I realized that I cared more for Nate's future than he did. Something was really wrong here. Something so distinctively evil had become a part of my son's life that even the shadow of the valley of prison didn't cause him concern. "They have programs there that will help the time go by quickly," he said matter-of-factly on the phone. The call was over and I had stopped crying. It would be a long time before I would cry again for my son.

## A New Endeavor

Shortly after the judicial system came into Idaho and swept my son to justice in Missouri, I was informed of his departure. I had made up my mind that once I heard Nate was gone, I would help inmates at our local county jail by bringing in a mentoring program. The local sheriff's staff had approved my involvement, once my own flesh and blood had left the premises. With Nate gone, I began going into the jail once a week. My plan was to have a Christ-centered mentoring meeting where I used scripture and helped men grow first as individuals and second as potential employees and businessmen—once they'd done their time.

Week after week I went in. At first just a trickle of male inmates showed up. Later, scores of men began attending. I needed assistance and found it in a group of very dedicated volunteers who helped man the weekly sessions with me. Eventually we were asked to do two services each week, and we had hundreds of men per month going through our program— which I called Band of Brothers, named after both Shakespeare's *Henry V* and the HBO miniseries about World War II. Each man who volunteered in jail month after month was a hero to me.

Some inmates remembered my son, but jail is a very rough-and-tumble place—with many inmates spending an average of only fourteen or so days behind bars—in comparison with prison, where inmates spend years. In a very short period of time, no one who attended our jail services knew who Nate was. And I was glad for that.

As time continued to pass, two white-collar inmates, who had extensive business backgrounds, asked me if I would be open to helping them start a staffed, safe, and sober housing business to enable ex-inmates to find stability. These houses would help those who were trying to overcome their addictions but needed a harbor of safe rest in which to succeed. In a very short period of time, a company was formed. Upon the two inmates' successful completion of their jail sentences, I invited them to become involved in the day-to-day activities of the company. None of us were drug addicts, and so none of us fully understood the long-term nature of what we'd started. I simply did not know what I did not know, so I asked a third ex-inmate who *did* have a background in drug abuse to join us in the start-up of this company. By faith in Christ, I moved forward. These three men joined me.

Eventually, all three men left the work, though the original idea lived on for a season. I gained a partner in Mac Mayer, who stepped in to help.

And that season brought much hope to ex-addicts, as well as a huge controversy to these kinds of communities.

Regulation of staffed, safe, and sober houses falls under the Americans with Disabilities Act. Ex-addicts who are in recovery are allowed to live in group homes, such as what we offered. The group homes, however, are normally single-family residences often located in normal neighborhoods. In Idaho there was no specific protocol for opening these legal homes; this allowed us the opportunity of simply receiving fire-department approval and then moving our clients in. In most cases, we had twelve men living in each five- or six-bedroom house; some houses were smaller and had fewer men living in them. We eventually opened three women's houses. The probation and parole system required that the ex-inmates work or be in constant search of work; hence, very few lingered at home each day.

Though our experience with Nate was key to helping Susan and me see the need for these houses, he was never the specific reason we began housing these ex-addicts. We wanted to help other people's family members. Oddly enough, early on, a member of Idaho's State Senate, John Andreason, was in a community leaders' meeting with me, to which I had been invited by the mayor of Boise. Much discussion occurred. After a prolonged silence, then-Senator Andreason said only one thing: "I'd like to thank you, Mr. Mansfield, for making money off your drug addict son's behavior with these houses." All were horrified.

Drug addicts and their families are often more disdained by people in authority than you'd believe.

I remember the moment when it became abundantly clear to me that I had to do something to help these people in need. One day, I was reading Isaiah, chapter 61, and I read where the Old Testament prophet wrote that the Messiah would come to "heal the broken hearted and to bring freedom to those who were in prison." It might seem a bit naïve in retrospect, but I sensed that ex-inmates and ex-addicts fell clearly into those two categories. Secondly, as I read Jesus' words in Nazareth, when he announced that He was the Messiah, I realized that He quoted from this same section of Isaiah 61. He was God on Earth and could have announced His entrance through a thousand other scripture passages, but He chose this specific one. Brokenhearted people and prisoners.

That was good enough for us. With the help of some key people, we kept the doors open, hoping that the cities and counties and state government would see that it was less expensive to have addicts at safe homes than it was to warehouse them in prisons with very little changes occurring except the turning of calendar pages. Our company lasted only four years.

## Letters from Nate

During this time, I received a letter from Nate. He said that he'd been in solitary confinement for four months and that during those months he had thought long and hard about his upbringing and where he had chosen to take his life—straight down the gutter. He asked us to forgive him and to welcome him back as a true son. He acknowledged his reliance on God and at the same time stated that prison life didn't allow much time for God, despite the many jailhouse conversions people read about.

On one hand, I was speechless at the clarity of thought he displayed in his writing, and on the other hand, I was seeing with my own eyes at our company how lives were indeed changing via jailhouse conversions. I appreciated his thoughts and introspections, though I did not agree with his sweeping generalizations. In short, I was glad for him, but I wanted to see more.

And yet, I still could not cry.

I did manage to laugh, though. Later in the year, I received another letter from Nate (again from solitary confinement . . . hmmm) in which he wrote:

*February 5th, 2005*
*Dad,*
    *Remember how you used to tell stories at nighttime . . . then stop; and Meg & I would make something up next?*
    *Well, I've been thinking about that for about four months and I finally decided to act. You'll know what it's about . . .*
    *I wrote four pages. It's now your turn.*
    *I don't care how much you write, but write at least a page.*
    *Please photocopy each page and send copies back to me. Also, send a copy of your part. Keep all the originals at the house.*
    *Maybe it will be good and we could sell it.*
    *It will give me something to look forward to (receiving it in the mail). And allow my need for an outlet to put words down on paper.*
    *Thanks Dad, let's write a kick-ass story.*
        *Love ya,*
        *Nate*

I couldn't help but laugh. Writing a book with Nate might be just as fun as when he was very little and we'd construct stories each evening at bedtime,

*And yet, I still could not cry.*

around objects that we would spy in his room. It was a tender and wonderful nighttime tradition that we implemented with all three of our children, and one I now do with my grandchildren.

In a true sense, Nate wanted to love me again—even at long distance; he chose the book idea to begin a dialogue between us. Though we never visited Nate in prison, we kept in contact with him by letters and phone calls. In many of those phone calls, he would tell me prison stories that ranged from the expected fight scenes to the occasional act of kindness.

Nate's letter included the first chapter of the book he wanted to write. I read it and was pleasantly surprised! His many hours of reading the world's best authors while incarcerated had acted as almost a college degree in writing well.

Nate's behavior was fascinating. He was a strong-willed, decisive, and direct man. Though shy and logical, he tended to be outspoken, stubborn, and demanding. Quite a contrast, indeed.

Two other qualities central to Nate's character were his toughness and his unyielding nature. Once, when accosted by a Missouri murderer in a Montgomery County Jail day room for simply sitting in a chair normally occupied by the killer, Nate's toughness let loose. Later, as he told me the story, his eyes twinkled. "Dad, you should have seen it. There I was in the day room watching TV, and this huge guy came up to me and said, 'Get outta my chair now, or I'll kill ya.'" Here's where Nate's eyes widened with glee, as he recounted the tale. He said, "Dad, I thought of all those days when I was younger and you taught me how to box with boxing gloves. I acted like I was getting out of this particular chair and as I bent down, I came up quickly with an upper cross that lifted this two-hundred-and-thirty-pound guy off his feet and onto the floor. I jumped on top

*In a true sense, Nate wanted to love me again.*

of him and wham-wham-wham, knocked him out. I knew I *had* to or this guy and others would order me around in that shark tank. Later the sheriff's deputies told me they often watched the videotape of that fight in their employees' lounge! Ha." Nate was indeed tough, unyielding, and had a twinkle in his eye.

These qualities combined to motivate my son to engage in challenging tasks that allowed him freedom to perform. He wanted to choose his tasks without input from others. He particularly liked opportunities to develop himself in a systematic way.

## Writing a Book with Nathan

And writing was one of those opportunities. His desire to revisit the cooperative storytelling of his youth took his strengths into account.

Upon receipt of Nate's February 5 letter, I found a quiet spot and began reading his first section of a thriller crime piece, which eventually took on the name *Death's Diamonds*.

In order to understand what was going through my mind as I read his first piece, a little background information is necessary. Nate was not a particularly strong student in his high school years. Maybe it stemmed from his early childhood learning difficulties, maybe it was part laziness, or maybe he simply saw high school as a time to enjoy friends, enduring classes and studies while doing so.

The idea of Nate becoming a writer was something far from anything I'd imagined.

And in a way he backed into it through reading.

While he was in county jail for a year, he spent his 365 days reading more than three hundred books. Today in my library at home, many of his books stand as silent reminders of the hours he spent escaping locked doors while learning from John Grisham, Stephen King, Mario Puzo, Tom Harris, Tim LaHaye, Jerry Jenkins, and so many other writers of national acclaim. Nate's hunger for reading fed his unknown ability to write. And he gained freedom in both areas.

So, his letters home became well worded and clearly laid out. They were not Ernest Hemingway masterpieces, but they were letters that Hemingway would have written home to his family: rich and colorful, moody and moving. They had a power to manipulate the emotions and to make the reader laugh. For my wife and me, they showed the growth in Nate and the difference between the present and the past.

*Nate wrestled with theological constructs, future dreams, and goals for himself.*

Nate honed his skill at communication. And we enjoyed his letters.

His letters home contained vignettes full of deep concern and focused questions. Many were commentaries on the happenings of those years—from the death of the pope to the political climate of post-9/11 America.

Nate wrestled with theological constructs, future dreams, and goals for himself. He saw the evil nature of drugs yet often wrote in his own journals of the love affair all addicts, including himself, have with them. Reading his journals—only after Nate's death—proved difficult for my wife and me. In the final analysis, though, they were also enlightening.

I slowly and methodically read Nate's first pages. I saw his characters come to life. Each had a purpose in the story; each had unique characteristics. In each of the characters, I saw people my son knew from prison. I could hear the language that surrounds the career of crime. Surprisingly missing were the F-bombs and raw conversational treatment of sexuality that so plays a part in the vocabulary of life amid and between inmates. It was a deft language of cultured, intelligent criminals.

And I found in these few pages a story of greed, avarice, and thievery.

I also realized that a backstory might be needed, so I began the process of writing the first chapter or phase of the story, allowing Nate's story to stand as the second chapter.

A father's creative prerogative, I suppose.

It turned out, Nate didn't seem to mind.

I wrote my additions, photocopied all the pages, and returned chapters one and two by mail.

Shortly thereafter, I received the third chapter of the story, along with a cover letter. Here is his cover letter, in part. Pardon the language and embrace the excitement.

> *Dad*
>
> *I just got the "story" . . . You can write! Connecting the Jewish businessmen and Italian mob perfectly fit, leaving questions asked . . .*
>
> *Giving [the main character] a believable come-from-nothing New York mobster feel . . . blew me away. Dad, it is so good.*
>
> *I kept repeating "damn" [and] "this man can write." I had the biggest smile on my face . . . and still do. You made my week. Man, it's good.*
>
> *I'm going to read it about twenty times and then write [the next chapter]. I want to make sure it connects with yours . . .*
>
> *Love,*
>
> *Nate*

*PS: Your foreshadowing is excellent. The second read was way better than the first! Love ya!*

Neither of us realized it at the time, but the process of writing this story would end up being less about the actual storyline and more about our conversations, our time writing together, and the reintroduction of Nate's childhood style of cooperative storytelling—allowing us to learn more about each other as adults. The result was like diamonds in settings of gold.

We simply had no idea how many of these precious diamonds we would share together in our lives.

Since the work on the first few chapters got us excited, we decided to just keep up the writing.

*Since the work on the first few chapters got us excited, we decided to just keep up the writing.*

The storyline was amazing. As I wrote, I had a smile on my face and hope in my heart. Together, we called the story *Death's Diamonds* because of the storyline, but I think God allowed us to call it that for what we would face in a very short while.

As a new author, Nate developed the lively adventure from the freedom of his mind, as his body sat behind heavy prison walls.

# Chapter Eleven

# Freedom

The book we wrote together took the remainder of Nate's time in prison. The exercise of coauthoring any article, research paper, or screenplay is, at best, a difficult and time-consuming undertaking. Ideally, the two authors work closely together, diplomatically speaking about possible plotlines or, even more important, one forcefully telling the other when some aspect of the piece is completely unacceptable.

Add thousands of miles, constrained time periods, the sheer depravity of Nate's living conditions, and the hope-denied atmosphere created by the chaos of incarceration, and the result could have been a long and tedious process for Nate and me. It was not that way at all. In fact, Nate and I had other correspondence that accompanied whatever the latest chapter was, and within that extra correspondence often were great notes of encouragement to each other.

## Nate Finds His Voice

Our fictional story of death and the greedy hunger of advancing past one's humble origins made the story come alive—just as the Nathan the Adventurer stories had come alive in our hearts and minds when Nate was younger. We each eagerly awaited the other's bulky letter that included the next segment of the story. Chapter after chapter was written. We were having a tremendous time together, occasionally even editing the storyline over the phone, when we had those few and precious moments.

In the complete isolation and quiet of solitary confinement, Nate found his voice through writing. His letters that accompanied the book drafts were well-written, pensive pieces that asked us about *our* lives— something long missing during his many years of drug addiction. He seemed to honestly care about his family. His letters were often replete with questions about the present and reflections on the past. Somehow, somewhere in the dark days of Nate's incarceration, he occasionally began to care for the well-being of others. A light of hope ignited in our hearts. Parents have a way of looking for hope in the most hopeless of situations, don't they?

*We were having a tremendous time together.*

And oftentimes, addicts or people users can spot that slight beam of hope in others and use it for their own selfishness. Having experienced so many years of heartbreak, Susan and I did not immediately show excessive hope to Nate. We thanked him for his letters, carefully wording our responses. We still felt an uncertainty in dealing with him. We waited for his next few letters to see if he would start asking us to help him with finances or contacts or . . .

We were determined to see him either own this newfound sensitivity or, if he was conning us, to stay in prison. Either way, we were starting a new relationship with our son that had nothing to do with him being an extension of us, but rather with him being a full and (we hoped) healthy individual, responsible for his own future.

## Release from Prison Approaching

Sadly, and against our strongest hopes, his addictive behavior of ups and downs continued to show itself. He was dry, but he was not sober. The book we were writing kept going back and forth between us; the chapters took interesting and unique twists. Yet his letters changed as he approached a possible release date. His counselor in prison had apparently recommended that he be given freedom, even shy of his first year. It was remarkable, and it was happening fast.

Soon the date was set for Nate's release. But one small yet significant item needed to be determined. Prior to prisoners being paroled they have to detail a home plan—a clear and concise strategic plan that will ensure that the inmate will not return to prison because of violations of their parole agreement. Nate called us at home and asked if he could be paroled back to Idaho—to our care and maintenance.

## Another Difficult Decision

It was a crossroads moment in all of our lives. He said he would involve himself in any substance abuse program in the state that we chose. His eagerness to return home was evident, but we were concerned with the specifics of what it would look like day to day. I asked if we could have a day or so to think and pray about it. Nate's prison counselor agreed to our pause, as did our son.

So began two of the most difficult days of decision in our lives. Susan and I speculated about what a future with Nate at our home would look like, given his past propensity to drift and cause chaos. We evaluated Nate's failure to take any substance abuse classes during his stay in both the local jail and later in prison. We considered our son's lack of interest in faith-based programs for his own self-awareness—he simply read his way through prison and cared little for the opportunities that presented themselves with pastors and lay leaders who volunteered daily around him.

We saw the benefit of having him live with us; our kids could all be reunited. Yet even in that possibility, I saw the need to keep Nate's possible future behavior away from his younger brother, Colin. Even driving in a car with ex-addicts and felons can pose problems for those without a criminal record. An innocent pull-over by a local policeman for a failed taillight could put Nate in prison the first time; having Colin in a car with Nate for a second pull-over was something from which I had to protect Colin. Drug addicts have spiritual radar for other substance abusers. Having Colin or Meg in a car with their older brother when, as was his custom, he might pick up a bad-news stranger was a potential problem I could avoid by one simple decision: saying no to him coming home to Idaho.

*Susan and I speculated about what a future with Nate at our home would look like.*

Also, in the past, Nate's sarcasm and rebellious attitudes had been like poisonous personality vapors that silently crept into the lives of his siblings. They loved their brother and naturally wanted to stand up for him when Susan and I were critical of something Nate had said or done. He didn't seem to have the same sarcastic wit any longer, and that gave us hope. We were tossed about in our decision making.

Yet Nate had burned us so badly for so long that we were exhausted. We had only so much energy left, as we were getting older. Ultimately, the parental duty of protecting our at-home thirteen-year-old son outweighed any further parental responsibility we could extend to our twenty-four-year-old son. We determined that our days of giving second chances to our oldest son were over; Nate was a man and we felt he had to bear the full weight of whatever faced him as he exited prison.

We called the prison back and told both Nate and his counselor no. He was devastated. We were liberated.

Though angry at us, Nate recovered and put together a home plan that placed him in a halfway house in Kansas City, Missouri. We did e-mail friends to ask if anyone knew of faith-based outreaches in Kansas City for sober ex-addicts. One of my friends from Southern California introduced us by e-mail to Melody Green, the musician Keith Green's widow. It was through that introduction that Nate and Melody became friends. When he was free, she invited him to her house for dinners with her friends and family members. Melody invited Nate to church and Bible study and he often joined her, though time regulations at the halfway house made this difficult.

## Nate Leaves Prison

An interesting anecdote about Nate as he left prison speaks volumes about the character he really always had. Footwear in prison is a coveted commodity. Good, expensive athletic shoes allow an inmate to play sports. In Nate's case it was basketball. He saved up the money that so many family members had put on the books for him at prison and bought a pair of comfortable Nike basketball shoes. He'd been asked to be on his cellblock's competitive basketball team. He was allowed to play and scored well. In a racially charged prison, Nate made friends with black teammates who not-so-kiddingly called him "Milk." First, some background.

I remember the excitement in his voice when he told me over the phone that the invitation to play came purely by accident. At first, as a white prisoner from Idaho, Nate was not well received by the black prison population. He was given the prison job of mowing the lawn and weeding, while black lifers played different sports, depending on what the season was. His tasks took him near the broken-down court where all the black lifers played basketball. Men who would never see the light of freedom in their lives sought value by playing a sports game they had learned as little boys.

Apparently, one afternoon while Nate was mowing the strip of lawn near the basketball asphalt, the warden called for one of the inmates who was engaged in a fierce game of b-ball. The head lifer, a black man in his early forties, yelled over at Nate: "Hey, Milk, you know how to play some basketball?" Nate nodded yes. "Then get your white ass over here and stand in for my main man. Don't get used to it, though. He'll be back in ten minutes." Nate told me that he joined this group of hard-core inmates, muscular from the years of lifting weights and competitive sports. Men who had no future on the outside and only had today to play ball, during their exercise breaks. They threw the ball to Nate.

What happened next is almost legend.

Nate put it this way to me when we met on that final weekend of his life: "Dad, it was like magic! I never played as good as I did that day. Every single three-point shot was successful. Most were swishes. Every layup I attempted, I made. I passed to others, and they made points. It was as if I was outside of my body watching an NBA player. The lifers just stood and stared. Then they smiled."

When the absent player presented himself and expected to quickly replace Milk, the head lifer shouted him down and told him to sit on the bench. "Milk stays, brother. He's one of us."

*"Dad, it was like magic! I never played as good as I did that day."*

Upon hearing this, I smiled the smile of a dad who had coached his son in many sports. He and I looked at each other, and it was as if he knew what I was thinking as I smiled. "Thanks, Dad, for coaching me all my life as a kid," Nate said. I couldn't answer; I simply held my tears and nodded my head. That puts the following in context.

The evening before his release from prison, Nate gave his athletic shoes to an inmate who had no shoes at all. Expecting that he would have his own original clothes available when he was discharged, he was rudely awakened to the reminder that he had been bused to Missouri from jail in Idaho in prison garb. He had no clothes. He had no shoes. The officers gave him discarded and wrinkled clothes from strangers. For his feet they gave him shower sandals. He hobbled out of prison in shower sandals.

He told me that with the money he had saved and gifts that were given to him from family that had gone into his prison account, he had enough to start his new life. The first thing he wanted to do was to buy a brand-new pair of really comfortable shoes.

As he exited the city bus that brought him to freedom, he was in downtown Kansas City. Nate told me later with tears in his eyes, "Dad, I got off the bus and just stood at a corner of the intersection. I was paralyzed. For the first time in years, I could walk in any direction, but here I was, stopped in my tracks. I could not make a decision as to which direction was the right one. I was alone. I knew no one, and it really didn't matter which direction I chose. Amid all these people getting on and off buses, it was the most alone I had ever felt, including solitary confinement."

Then, he broke from the difficult memory and suddenly laughed. "Hey, Daddio, I took what I knew would always be the correct direction for a conservative. I went right . . . and found a shoe store. Wouldn't you know it!" We both laughed through our sadness. Later he drove me past that bus stop, a sacred place of remembrance for him.

Nate as a free man was something to behold. Soon he achieved peace in his life. He made friends with professional people. He got a job, found a place to live, and was open to improving his new life. Susan and I remained involved in Nate's life but not too involved. He had the freedom of calling us and talking anytime he wanted to. We had the freedom of suggesting possible opportunities to him, and he would either accept or reject them. Slowly, we began setting healthy boundaries, and it felt great.

# A Surprise Visit

As promised, in December, just weeks after his release, I visited Nate in Kansas City. It was a visit that he expected but one that actually sort of came in the form of a surprise! He had not sought our advice years before when he began his trans-state drug use, and we felt he needed to breathe the free air of his newly adopted state by himself. I was coming to visit him, not to give him advice. People at the time needlessly commended us for exercising "tough love" on Nate. *Nonsense.* Tough love is what we'd spent a lifetime doing with him. Somehow, tough love never worked on Nate. No, it was not tough love, it was simply self-preservation as a family. Nate had to grow up; so did we.

Susan and I knew that Nate would need help in adjusting to his new life of freedom, but not from us. In 2004, Susan and I had attended an experiential eleven-day seminar called Focus (not associated with Focus on the Family) and had profited greatly from it. Personal coaching and additional insight is a valuable help to people interested in changing, and that was us. We knew that Nate was also interested in changing, so we paid for him to attend a seminar near his new home in Missouri.

*It was not tough love, it was simply self-preservation as a family. Nate had to grow up; so did we.*

Begun in 1990 by "Dr. Phil" McGraw, his brother Joe, and their then business partner Wayne McKamie, Focus had its home in Kansas City. In time, Dr. Phil went on to *Oprah Winfrey Show* fame, and Wayne continued helping people one small group at a time (Focusseminar.com). The Focus program was expanded to Boise in late 2003 (EmpowerBoise.com), and we attended in the spring of 2004, gaining a great deal of freedom as a couple. Having gone through it in our own hometown in Idaho showed us the advantage of Nate staying near home in Kansas City for his seminar.

Prior to Nate's release from prison, I mentioned to Melody Green that Nate had agreed to go through the Focus Seminar training. She was intrigued. When it came time for Nate to attend, he did so without any feelings of coercion from Susan or me. My December trip to see him coincided with his graduation from the seminar. I asked Melody if she'd like to join me in surprising Nate at his graduation. She answered yes, and we plotted a fun way to show up.

As parents and friends flooded into the graduation ceremony, we hid behind a bunch of people. Nate was looking around, stretching his neck to see if anyone had come for him. Suddenly our eyes met. Nate loved seeing Melody and me together as we popped out of nowhere to surprise him and encourage him in this new phase of his life. Melody was so sweet to care for my son. She told me that Nate's passion reminded her of her late husband's honesty, energy, and charisma. Nate was twenty-four years old. Keith passed away when he was twenty-eight.

After the Focus Seminar training graduation, Melody invited Nate and me to her home for an early dinner and a time to sit and talk. Driving over by ourselves to her very lovely and modest home in Kansas City, Nate told me in the rental car, "Dad, I know you loved Keith Green's music, and I know he helped you grow as a young Christian. I asked Melody if she wouldn't mind taking you to the part of the house that has all his instruments, awards, and pictures. Melody said she'd love

*Nate loved seeing Melody and me together as we popped out of nowhere to surprise him.*

to, so we're gonna have some time there, Daddio." Nate could not have arranged a nicer, more meaningful gift for me. I loved how he called me by that nickname whenever he was excited or when he was lightheartedly teasing me.

Melody greeted us at her door and showed us around her home; we had a lovely meal together that afternoon. She told us about the young girls she had been mentoring who were living in her home. We met one young lady, who was glowing with her newfound faith in Jesus. You could tell she was enjoying life. Melody gave me two autographed copies of her book *No Compromise*—one inscribed to me, the other, by Nate's suggestion, to his brother, Colin. Then she asked if we'd like to see her special memorabilia area dedicated to Keith's life.

Nate led the way. I can't describe the honor I felt in entering the room that housed Keith's grand piano, his many guitars, and an amazing array of family photos and album covers, hung nicely on the wall. It was a somber moment for me. I stood quietly and looked all around.

I remembered back to 1979, lying in bed with my bride on that Sunday morning as Keith's haunting lyrics moved me to grow up.

*Jesus rose from the grave*
*And you, you can't even get out of bed.*

I saw wonderful photos of Keith and his children. Melody pointed out one picture in particular: it was of Keith and their two children who perished in the terrible plane accident in 1982. "That's Josiah and that's Bethany," Melody said. "They were wonderful children, really wonderful."

Just a few years later, I reflected back on Melody's heart—the heart of a mother who lost two children—when I looked into the eyes of my own wife, Susan, during Nate's memorial service. Both women had the tired, tender eyes of mothers who deeply loved their children and missed them so painfully, no matter how many days or years had elapsed.

Melody asked me if I'd like her to play one of my favorite songs written by her husband. I think I surprised her at first with my answer. I quietly told her, "No, but may I ask a different favor instead?" She nodded. "Would you play one of my favorites that *you* wrote and Keith recorded? Your song 'There Is a Redeemer'?" She quietly smiled and found the CD.

The opening chords of the song somberly met the three of us as we stood and grasped hands facing the large speakers. As we listened, we closed our eyes; we opened our hearts.

*As I held Nate's hand in mine, never did I consider the tragedy that we would eventually face.*

As the song ended, I was sobbing. I held Melody's hand in my right hand and Nate's hand in my left. My body was shaking convulsively, and I wondered how terrible it was for Melody to have lost in death those young ones she dearly loved, all the while continuing to live and grow older, serving Christ.

As I held Nate's hand in mine, never did I consider the tragedy that we would eventually face.

Nate attended various events with Melody at her church, as time allowed. It was a condensed but important time period in Nate's life; Melody Green blessed my son. She blessed my whole family by caring for my son. When Nate passed away, Melody sent us a heartfelt letter of condolence.

# A Letter from Melody

*Dear Dennis and Family,*

*I returned late Sunday night from Charlotte, to receive your note yesterday.*

*I am so very sad to hear of Nate's death, which is such a great tragedy and tremendous loss.*

*I am deeply saddened too. I really liked Nate and saw so much potential and such a tender heart in him. But he was torn . . . in the valley of decision.*

*I remember our dinner and the time at my home. Nate and I spoke a few times after. It took many phone calls to try to set his schedule so he could come to church with me. He was so drawn to what he knew was good and right, but other forces had a strong grip.*

*Your questions, second-guessing, and utter devastation are only natural and will persist for a while.*

*From what I saw, I believe you did everything you could, with the best of intentions, to help set your son on another course.*

*You are suffering more than words can possibly explain and I understand. It will take a while. Nate's death will bring many to new life, although today that's probably not a great consolation . . . much better to have seen Nate come into a new life himself. But in the years to come, it will be very*

*"But in the years to come, it will be very meaningful for your family to see Nate's story change the stories of the lives of other young men and women."*

147

*meaningful for your family to see Nate's story change the stories of the lives of other young men and women.*

*But for now, I know the grace of God will descend like a cloud over you and your family. God WILL carry you through this season of grieving. It will not be short. Let it pour out and be what it is.*

*However, it won't be forever either. Life will go on, love will go on, and lives will be changed forever—especially yours.*

*May you and your family remember to love each other, give room and grace, and don't try to place any blame anywhere. Stay close to your wife in open communication . . . don't drift or isolate from each other. Everyone has their own journey in these times but all can unify in the great loss of Nate the son, and Nate the brother.*

*God is faithful and will carry you through. He is good and He loves you. Be assured that Jesus is with you and is utterly heart-broken as well.*

> *I am so very very sorry.*
> *With all my love,*
> *Melody*

Melody's kind words of a wife and mother who had loved and lost her husband and two children deeply touched my father's heart.

## Nate and Ginny

In Missouri, Nate eventually fell in love with a very kind and determined young professional woman, Ginger, whom we called Ginny—my mom's name. Ginny is a college graduate. They were together for three years, planning eventually to be married. I remember thinking how proud my mom would have been to have another Ginny Mansfield in the family.

For Nate's twenty-seventh birthday, Susan and I were invited to Missouri to be with Nate and Ginny. The trip was generally very positive, allowing us to see where and how Nate was living. There were aspects, though, that caused us to be concerned. His speech was slurred—a sure sign of drug use—and he seemed distracted. Nate leveled with us that he was seeing a doctor and that he was, indeed, using prescription opiates, under that doctor's care, for a recent back injury. Even with that "acceptable" mantle, Nate was high at times during our visit. Licensed doctors, legal pharmaceutical drugs, and ex-addicts—this is a recipe for disaster.

Seeing the impact of any drugs on Nate's life made us sad. The slippery slope of prescription pills on the behavior of a recovering drug addict is steep.

Even after we expressed our concern, Nate seemed to really want us to be with him—meeting his friends, seeing the sights of Kansas City, visiting an art museum in Kansas City, seeing van Gogh paintings, visiting the Harry S. Truman Library, taking in a Royals game, eating dinner at the world-famous Arthur Bryant's Barbeque. Then in the evening, we'd sit and talk.

One night, Ginny took us on a drive through some of the really beautiful neighborhoods of Kansas City. Nate was seeing some friends, so just the three of us climbed into her SUV. We would meet Nate in a couple of hours. Apparently, the city is known worldwide for its fountains in the summer and its amazing seasonal light display at Christmastime. On this hot summer night, the fountains seemed quite welcoming and appeared everywhere. I've never seen so many outdoor fountains in my life.

As we drove through a particular residential neighborhood, not far from where Ginny's house was located, she pointed to a house that had obviously had fire damage. "See that house?" Ginny stated matter-of-factly. "Nate was walking his dog down that street a few weeks back and saw it was on fire. The fire department had not yet arrived. People could see activity in the upstairs window. They just stood there; not Nate. He quickly tied up Satchel, ran to the front porch of the house, and kicked down the door, looking for people and animals upstairs. The family was not there, but their dog was and Nate rescued it from the flames." Then she drove on to the next site as if this was just a normal thing.

I was blown away, but I shouldn't have been. That was Nate's heart. Nate never told us about his act of bravery.

Two other evenings, in particular, also stand out as amazing to me. Both times Susan and I had retired to our guest room when we heard a knock at the door. Both evenings it was Nate. He asked if he could come in and pray with us as we went to bed.

The first time it happened, I was stunned and a bit speechless. "Sure, Nate, uh, um . . . come on in," was about all I could muster as a response. He knelt down next to our bed and began to pray, thanking God for us as his parents, for our visit with him, and for the many things that we had taught him in his youth. His prayer was personal, sincere, and caring. He was talking to his heavenly Papa about his mom and dad. We were honored to listen in while praying with him. We prayed for him as well, honestly thanking God for giving us our son, our beautiful Nate. When he departed that first night, Susan and I clung to each other and cried. Nate's love for God was real, even with his

*"The family was not there, but their dog was and Nate rescued it from the flames."*

many years of drug addiction, his times of incarceration, and his separation from his family. The second evening of prayer was just as precious.

July 14, 2008, was Nate's birthday. It was exactly twenty-seven years earlier when Susan delivered our first child, when Harry Chapin's music made me weep, when I decided to love our brand-new son intentionally, when it all began. It was the anniversary of the first day we saw our son as a baby—and it was a reminder of how deeply touched I had been by John Lennon's song "Beautiful Boy."

Just as Lennon had sung, I had been patient and so had Nate. And there we were, seeing him come of age. It was a sweet moment in our lives. Susan and I saw our son as a man, not as a boy.

And that was also the last day Susan saw our son alive.

But not me.

## A Final Meeting with Nate

A few months later, a winter business trip took me to Branson, Missouri. I was hopeful that Nate might swing down from Kansas City to Branson and possibly spend a few hours with me. In God's providence, something even greater happened.

My flight was to take me from my hometown of Boise to a stopover in Denver and then from Denver to the local airport near Branson. As I disembarked from the plane in Denver, the gate representative told me that due to my arriving later than planned, I had just missed the connecting flight. I was directed to their customer service desk to make new plans.

Whenever schedules change by chance, I've learned to look for God's fingerprints on the situation; this one seemed to have God's fingerprints all over it. As I approached the customer service rep, I asked one simple question: "Though it's not where I originally planned on landing, is it possible for you to have me fly into Kansas City's airport tonight?" She paused and then asked me why. I told her of Nate's arrests, his addictions, and his recovery and that he lived in Kansas City and just might be able to drive me down to Branson, if I could reach him and ask. She smiled and looked from side to side. Shyly she said to me, "I'm a recovering substance abuser—and I'd love to help you. I'm going to give you four extra days with your son in Kansas City, okay?" I was thrilled. Angelic help in an airline uniform! I called my son, and Nate responded with a hoot and this: "Daddio, I would *love* to have time with you. I'll meet you at whatever time you arrive!"

The customer service rep put me on a plane to Kansas City, and Nate met me at midnight. That was good enough for Nate.

He and Ginny planned the road trip that immediately faced the two of us. We also had the next several days to be together. It was fantastic. The road trip allowed Nate and me to just talk—as we did on so many road trips during his youth. We talked about fun movies and fun times; we shared our thoughts about future plans and the book we had written together, *Death's Diamonds*. He reiterated how he couldn't wait to see it published.

Around 3:00 a.m., we stopped and went into a convenience store. Nate greeting the night-shift worker with a fun-loving, "Hi, pal!" The man, named Dennis, took time with us and told us his life story. He'd been, as we say in Idaho, "rode hard and put away wet" and looked like a man in his late sixties, though he told us he was forty-two. Prison, drugs, and *many* uncomfortably bad decisions had brought him to this job at this time in the morning. And Nate listened to him. Really listened. I watched as my son ministered to this broken man with a sadly misshapen life. Nate asked him about himself. And Dennis joyously talked with my son. I simply stood and watched for almost forty-five minutes. It was beautiful to behold, then and now. Nate seemed to be looking at himself.

We made it to Branson, Missouri, at 7:00 a.m. for a meeting with Gary and Norma Smalley, their staff, and my friend and client Michael Boerner. Their ministry has been housed in Branson for quite a few years. Nate stayed at the hotel, and I went to our meeting. The day went well. Michael, who had organized the meeting, had us in a beautiful five-star hotel. Michael had seen Nate grow up; he had known him since Nate was in the fourth grade. He told Nate to order room service. "Anything you want, order," he said. Nate told me later that night, "Dad, until today I've *never* had room service in my life! I ordered two meals and ate like a king! They brought me food to my room and I watched ESPN all day. Think of that! *Me! Room service!*" I stood smiling with Nate at his good fortune, wondering to myself how far away his years behind bars felt to him at this moment. His innocence was so refreshing. His appreciation was so real. This was my beloved son in whom I was well pleased.

The time with Gary and Norma Smalley was a productive day-long brainstorming session, reviewing the ways their international ministry could help those who were thinking of divorce as a solution to their pain. Gary is a wonderful man whose care and concern for people knows no bounds. Norma is a gracious and strong leader who has a deep concern for the incarcerated in her local county. During breaks that day, she and I *I watched as my son ministered to this broken man with a sadly misshapen life.* talked about my family's response to Nate's time in jail and prison. I was taken by Norma's incredibly kind attitude toward

Nate, though she had not met him. She *knew* what I was talking about. Gary's son, Michael, was in attendance at the meeting, and he and I also had some deep discussion about Nate. Later, after Nate passed away, Michael came by Boise on business and stayed the night at our home, befriending our other son, Colin. I will never forget the laughter and love of the entire Smalley family.

We finished our official business the next day and made our way back to Kansas City. For the next three days, Nate and I spent almost every waking hour talking, laughing, and watching movies from his incredible collection of DVDs. We watched his favorite movies and ate world-famous Arthur Bryant's Kansas City barbecue and laughed till we could not laugh anymore. The last evening of my stay at his house, we didn't go to bed. We stayed up the entire night. He had me watch his favorite five or so movies. It was part of our mutual family culture to watch movies together—and this seemed so fitting. He was teaching me through film.

Occasionally we'd take stretch breaks and drive around. His fiancée, Ginny, joined us as well. It was the most remarkable time together since Susan and I had been with Nate earlier in the year for his birthday.

Driving around Kansas City with Nate and Ginger during my surprise stay helped me see my son's life as it was being lived out daily. We just did normal things together. We talked and laughed, ate, and told stories on one another—and laughed some more. We discussed politics and Nate gave me his thoughts on the newly sworn-in president, Barack Obama. Nate didn't like the fact that a "true" conservative had not been on the ballot against U.S. senator Obama.

I asked him about his own opinion on the legalization of marijuana—checking to see if he had changed his thinking. At first he took the typical "hemp" line that "it's not addictive," and he was surprised when I agreed with him. I then asked him whether there was anything in marijuana use that contributed to a culture of addiction for those who moved on to drugs like heroin and other opiates. He paused and then in an amazing moment of openness said this: "You know, Dad, there is. The people you hang out with have a way of taking you to areas that you never thought about before." I just nodded my head and said, "Hmm, I see your point." Nothing else needed to be said. Nate was seeing the pitfalls himself for the first time. He

> *"The people you hang out with have a way of taking you to areas that you never thought about before."*

acknowledged his friends' behavior but seemed either unwilling to confront them or incapable of it. Even while I was there at his home, there was evidence of prescription drug abuse.

The next day, Nate and Ginny raced me to the airport and bought me a hot chocolate at Starbucks while I was checking myself in. Nate knew I'm a hot chocolate lover, and this was to be his final gift to me. I kissed him on the lips and quickly hugged his neck, thanking both of them for the time spent together. Nate hugged me with his longer-than-life muscular arms. I can still feel that hug.

He was unshaven and had a baseball cap on and a Dr Pepper in his hand. "Dad, if you have *any* problems with the flight, call and I'll come get you," he said. They were words that so many of us say when we drop off loved ones at an airport. Then he added, "Dad, I love ya. I always have. I always will." And he smiled that cockeyed smile of his and kissed me on the lips, again. My last words to him, face-to-face, were, "Nater, I love you, too." He turned and in a moment was gone. He returned to his car, which was parked illegally at the curb. I chuckled to myself: *Nate, Nate, Nate.* My last image of him alive was as he jumped in his car with Ginny and drove away with the radio blaring an oldies station. I remember wondering if Harry Chapin's "Cat's in the Cradle" was playing on his car radio.

# Chapter Twelve

# Nate's New Life

Shortly before Nate died, I was asked to speak at a church—one in which Nate grew up as a child. They knew my family. They knew my son.

I did not know it at the time, but Nate had just been arrested for what would be the last time, for a parole violation: driving a vehicle to a meeting with his parole officer. He would spend forty-one days behind bars as he waited for a decision by the parole board regarding his possible release. These would be forty-one of the last forty-three days of his life.

## *The Prideful Older Brother*

During that sermon, I used the prodigal son parable to address how, in many ways and over the years, I had acted like the older brother each time Nate squandered what the Lord gave him. I published a piece about it on my blog. Here's a snippet from my comments:

> Many of us use the term "prodigal son," often not knowing, fully knowing, what it means. Many believe that the story involves just a good dad and a bad son.
>
> We often forget that there is a third party in the story . . . the older son. The prideful son. The older son whose life was well lived was so angry at both the dad and the younger, prodigal son for the grace extended. He himself was "clean." His brother was "dirty." It is a painfully real presentation about my own anger and . . . hypocrisy. Instead of seeing myself as the good dad who was awaiting his bad prodigal son, I finally saw myself as the prideful older brother.

The full presentation that I gave at that church was put on their website. Nate's fiancée, Ginny, listened to it and had Nate listen to it over the phone, while he sat in prison. He was released shortly afterward.

## A Powerful Conversation

Monday, March 9, 2009, was the last conversation I had with Nate—ever. We talked by phone. It was just before lunch, and we talked for an hour and half. It was a confusing call. And it was a powerful time of healing discussion. It started with Nate being angry that I had spoken at our old church, that my message had been recorded, and that the recording was on the Internet—he didn't feel that others needed to be told things about his life. Ever the reserved person, he simply felt it was his business and not theirs. He did not want to be judged by them. He was really angry at one of the conflict examples I had used from his time in prison. "It's *my* story, Dad, not yours!" he yelled into the telephone receiver. Equally as forceful, I reminded him that his recent life's journey had affected our entire family—and it wasn't for the good. The temperature rose between us to volcanic levels. I screamed into the speaker, "It's not just *your* story, Nate. Your life took all of us down into the pit." He never backed down. Neither did I. The intensity grew. Screaming sentences overlapped screaming sentences. The anger was intense. My business partner, Mac Mayer, got up from his desk next to mine and quietly left our office.

The first forty-five minutes of the conversation saw Nate and me air our deepest anger

*He never backed down. Neither did I. The intensity grew.*

at each other. We were harsh and unrelenting. *Every* piece of dirty laundry was brought out.

Then, as if we were exhausted and could go no further in anger, we moved toward love and forgiveness. The second forty-five minutes of talking was a time of deep respect. We did not raise our voices and did not talk over each other. We talked with love in our voices for each other.

The last words I shared with my son were the same last words I received from him: "I love you."

We both said it, and we both meant it.

I hung up the phone and immediately understood what had just happened between my son and myself. We were healed.

## Nate's Final Days

Almost forty-eight hours from that very conversation, Nate went to be with the Lord.

We found out later that on Tuesday, March 10, 2009, Nate had applied for a job, which he got. He interviewed well and saw it as a step up as he and Ginny planned their future together. I am not aware of what else happened on the afternoon and evening of the tenth, except that Ginny cooked some food that night and Nate enjoyed what he had apparently not had during his most recent incarceration: bacon on the griddle.

At noon on Wednesday, March 11, 2009, my wife and daughter received a frantic phone call from Ginny during their Bible study. Nate was ill or in trouble, Susan could not quite tell, since Ginny was crying and screaming on the phone.

The Kansas City paramedics were working on Nate on the floor of his bedroom with his shirt off, and all medical personnel were at peak performance. While Susan listened on the phone, they came on the line to talk to her. They had just that minute pronounced him dead.

Our beautiful, beautiful Nate was no more.

Many weeks later the toxicological report came to us. Our son died in his sleep of adverse drug reactions—two drugs in trace amounts interacting with each other, causing his death. It was not an overdose.

*Two drugs in trace amounts interacting with each other, causing his death. It was not an overdose.*

Nate told me during the healing portion of that last phone conversation that during his forty-one days behind bars he was put in a cell with a chaplain from the Missouri prison system who was also a felon and had violated his own parole. Nate and this man spent forty-one days behind bars with no TV, no other inmates, no programs, and nothing to do except talk and read the only book that was in their cell: the Bible. It was during those precious captive days that Nate reconnected with his faith in a far deeper way than ever before. Nate always had tough questions for Bible teachers, and he was often left empty by their hollow answers to his specifically difficult queries. This chaplain/cellmate answered all of them, Nate told me upon his release. He said he finally "got it."

From that, I learned that it was good having my "child" arrested so that he could finally and tearfully "get it" as an adult. I learned that God doesn't need me to help Him with His son or daughter.

I am *also* learning that being "in process" is a place where God wants us—sure of Him but not so sure of our parenting and ourselves. The not knowing amid chaos demands that we move into Him. The losses of business and respect, even the ability to provide daily bread for our families, demand a deeper understanding that we are God's children and He really will provide for us—all of us, including our children. Even unto death.

It was said many years ago, "God has no grandchildren." That is correct. He loves our children more than we do because they are His.

I've learned that it's okay to keep depending on the Lord. When the plentiful times come, contentment must rest in blessing the name of the Lord. And when the times of failure arrive, the same contentment must be sought after with the knowledge that, as Job says in chapter 1, verse 21, "The Lord gives and the Lord takes away; blessed be the name of the Lord."

I have chosen to bless the Lord at the deepest and most painful time of my life.

# Chapter Thirteen

# Heaven

$A$ couple of Sundays after our son died, I heard a bulletin item being read from the church pulpit—my home church was planning a men's retreat. God's voice spoke instantly to me: "Go." I've come to know His voice; our son's recent death had ramped up both the volume and the frequency of the Lord's voice to my spirit. It was clear. There was no mistaking it—God wanted me to go to this retreat.

## *Obeying God's Voice*

I simply said, "Okay, Lord," and turned to my wife, Susan. "I'm going to attend that men's retreat." She looked surprised because she knew that I had long ago quit attending these types of retreats. I'd come to see them as near-fake mountain-top experiences for men who returned home only to live their failed lives as though a savior wasn't really needed. In many ways, having spoken at such men's movement events in the past was deeply disappointing to me. No wonder Susan was so surprised! I was equally surprised.

But I went. Two friends, Kevin Hearon and Bill Proctor, and I drove to the event and had a sweet time of discussion; we reminisced about Nate. It seemed as if the drive was being held on a celestial plane. My two friends had known my son since he was ten years old. Both men loved him and saw the devastation that his life of drugs had brought us—and the equal devastation that came from his death. To rejoice with them about the happier and more fulfilling times in my son's life was tremendous. We arrived at the retreat in the beautiful mountains of Idaho that evening. It was a little slice of Heaven on earth. I'd come to understand that Idaho in any season may well be the doorstep to Heaven.

But I'd not seen *anything* yet.

The next morning I awoke early so that I could attend the worship session being led by the nationally known worship leader Andy Hendley. It was especially meaningful, since, at our request, Andy had performed at Nate's funeral just a month earlier. He had sung, among other things, Melody and Keith Green's "There Is a Redeemer."

At the men's retreat, I found a padded chair in a long row and sat alone with eyes closed, singing lyrics to the well-known music Andy played. As can be the case with certain worship leaders, when the lyrics run their course and are completed, the music leader can choose to continue the chords and those individuals worshipping God are encouraged to sing out other lyrics or praises or whatever may be on their hearts. At times, it can be a wonderfully orchestrated cacophony of noise unto the Lord.

Such was the case that Saturday morning with Andy. Though my expression of worshipful Christianity had not often included this type of singing experience, I decided to flow more freely and open my mouth. It wasn't my normal style, but I did it anyway.

## Transported in the Spirit

What I experienced is almost unexplainable. As I opened my mouth, I lost control of my voice. The Holy Spirit began singing to me, using my own lips and tongue. It was not what many of us have either experienced or seen as the gift of tongues. It was the Holy Spirit singing to me in my own voice. He sang about my son Nate. The lyrics were straightforward and amazing. He spoke of how He was with my son completely to the end and that Nate's death was not painful. I heard words that I had never spoken myself, describing what my son saw as he entered Heaven.

I must either be a bit slow or unable to allow my imagination to picture what the Holy Spirit sang to me, because I didn't quite get what was being described. Maybe it was how the message was being delivered. Try as I could, I was unable to picture it in my mind. Apparently the Holy Spirit knew this and acted. The music in my ears faded away . . .

I suddenly found myself on the outskirts of a city with an ancient, looming gate attached to a wall of immense size. The gate was open and bright light was emanating from behind the gate. Something was in the way, though.

I was looking at a silhouetted back image of a man; the brightest light I had ever experienced emanated from

*I suddenly found myself on the outskirts of a city with an ancient, looming gate attached to a wall of immense size.*

the open city gate and framed his body. I knew as only a parent can know that this silhouetted image was my son, staring away from me and toward the incredible intense light in front of him. My eyes were at a little child's height; apparently I was seated somehow. I was able to view Nate as he stood at his full stature of six feet four inches. I slowly moved on a swivel, somehow in this seated position; my perspective changed from his back, moving around his right side to directly in front of him. I could see Nate; I could actually see my son, tall as ever, yet he could not see me. In fact, he was focusing on something above me—he was looking toward the source of the bright light, now directly behind me. It was Heaven. Though I knew this to be true, I didn't look over my shoulder, as I did not want to miss one second of looking at my son.

He was healthy and beaming; his complexion and hair were shining. He wore the same type of clothes he'd worn on Earth—a T-shirt, jeans, an open long-sleeve flannel shirt, and his signature brownish baseball cap, tipped up ever so slightly, allowing me to see his face. His mouth was in a huge smile, and I could see his teeth, all straight and returned to their original predrug, pre-tobacco days. Even a noticeable childhood nick on his front right tooth existed no longer. Nate's body was perfectly lean, muscular, and full of health.

Nate smiled his cockeyed smile—a mixture of joy and embarrassment—and stood long enough for me to focus on his face and record in my mind the last (and first!) best picture of Nathan Dennis Mansfield, one that his "Daddio" could memorize and, in the future, replay over and over again.

Then I heard my son's voice. Still smiling, he opened his mouth, and said, "This is just like Mom and Dad said." He walked forward toward me and toward the illuminated heavenly gate behind me, then my son traveled right through me, as if I were a translucent image. He was gone.

And my visit to God's holy hill ended in a snap of a finger. In the blink of an eye, in the final smiling sentence of my son, I knew that Nate was now in the presence of his heavenly Father—that God joyously welcomed home *His* beautiful Nate. And that in his heavenly home were some very special sofas that had long ago been sent ahead.

## Dark Times, Brilliant Diamonds

After that experience, I came home and bought the single best book on eternity: *Heaven* by Randy Alcorn. The book has changed my perspective of this earth and the current Heaven; Heaven is yet to unfold on the New Earth. It is simply a must read.

I've learned that what may appear to be the darkest times of our lives may simply be the background against which God is showing Himself to be the brightest of brilliant gems.

Never in the decade plus of drug abuse, broken family relationships, failed career paths, utter chaos, and finally unbelievable pain when Nate died could I have imagined that the dark black cloth that hung over us was a backdrop for the diamonds of a better, more real life.

*The dark black cloth that hung over us was a backdrop for the diamonds of a better, more real life.*

When Nate and I penned our book, *Death's Diamonds*, I had no intention of writing the book you are holding, yet this book came as a result of writing *Death's Diamonds*. This book was simply a written extension of a father's nighttime storytelling method, expressing the love of a son for his father and the love of a dad for his child.

*Beautiful Nate* is written out of deeply painful experiences that I neither wanted for my family nor would want for others—unless your times of pain and mourning point toward hope, the real hope that is found in Jesus Christ.

It is my desire, based on that hope, that you are encouraged during your current time of distress and loss.

Though yours may right now be a life where your bright dreams have faded into a background of death, please hold firm to the fact that life's true diamonds are yet to shine. The best in your life has not yet come your way.

*Chapter Fourteen*

# Death's Diamonds

At the publishing of this book, it will be four years since Nate died. The deep grief of learning of his death, preparing for the funeral, celebrating his life at the memorial (which can still be viewed on Vimeo), burying him, and finally walking through the deep daily distress of loss have all been passing away. Though they'll never be completely absent from my life, or the lives of my family, the intensity of the emotions are simply diminishing through time, as Melody said they would.

## *The Reality of Loss*

Just as life is a process, so is grief. The birth of a child and the death of that child are purely events—epic crossroads for families entrusted with such joy or pain. Yet, it's the act of *process* that more fully fills in the actual day-to-day happenings of life.

*169*

As I've talked about in earlier chapters, Nate and I wrote a book titled *Death's Diamonds* during a time when he was not doing very well and was in solitary confinement in prison. Within that fictional storyline is a young man who grew up under the caring watch of a loving grandmother. Through a series of twists and turns the life that the main character wanted—and the life each of us wants—was stripped down to its essentials. Like brilliantly white diamonds against the blackest of backgrounds, the importance of love shines in contrast to the worst of unlovely times.

I've presented the example of losing my son as an active metaphor for the many, many things in all of our lives that simply do not go in our favor. Loss is a horrible thing through which many of us may travel and some of us must travel. It's a part of life, and yet when we are the ones experiencing that loss, we sometimes think the pain is unique to us. Winning is expected but losing is not?

How absurd. Loss is a part of life.

*Like brilliantly white diamonds against the blackest of backgrounds, the importance of love shines in contrast to the worst of unlovely times.*

## One Man's Story

I know a young man who lost often. He came from a mother and father who should never have married. The dad was often brutal to his young children, then loving—the product of an angry alcoholic mother and a quiet father. Harsh words, then vacations, then slaps across the face, smiles, then punches and constant belittling. These characteristics were passed through the generations until the young man chose differently.

Yet the young man chose to find a life different from his angry father's.

The young man's mother was loving and caring but weak and dependent on prescription drugs. She offered no protection against the violent actions of the father. The siblings banded together like soldiers against a common enemy. The only true victories were when each child left home.

And the young man grew, believing that anything was possible. From elementary school through secondary school he succeeded. Grades, sports, and friends were his. Honors and accolades surrounded him at high school graduation.

Though to others, the father spoke glowingly about his son (and his other children), he never blessed any of them to their faces until he was an old man. "It isn't his style to encourage," the ill mother often told the kids.

And the young man shot for the stars, encouraging others as he proceeded along. Receiving a four-year scholarship to a prestigious East Coast school, he was soon elected president of his class. Then, as a twenty-year-old, he began to lose.

His parents divorced during his sophomore year. His scholarship was taken away after two years, because of his poor grades.

He was readmitted to a smaller college on probation and was almost asked to leave the new college when his GPA didn't rise quickly. Only the help of a kind professor kept him there. After graduation, he was selected to run the press activities for a U.S. Congress race. The candidate lost.

Along the way, at age twenty-two, he surrendered his life to Christ.

Two years later, he himself ran for U.S. Congress at the age of twenty-four and lost. He ran again for office at twenty-six and lost.

He opened a mortgage company when interest rates were 20 percent. It folded.

*He got up, time and time again, dusting himself off and looking to the Lord for his value.*

He started other companies, garnering some success and more than his share of failures.

He was felled often by failure. Yet he got up. He ran for elected office half a dozen times in thirty years and lost every one of them.

And he got up, time and time again, dusting himself off and looking to the Lord for his value.

He was known as a key family-values political leader in the nation; yet he had a son who was addicted to heroin and died. His company that helped ex-addicts lost its funding and closed.

You know who this man is, for I am he.

And to some extent, this man is *every* person reading this book who has failed but is not a failure. Men and women, adults and teens, we are people who lose and lose again—quietly hoping no one notices, so we can keep on pretending that everything's all right. We quietly mask our failures and overplay our meager successes. Loss can, if we let it, become a powerful teacher who shares precious life lessons that will never be forgotten.

## Nate's Influence Lives On

Nate's death was a tragedy. Our two great friends and former business partners, Mac and Dianne Mayer, changed our perspective on

Nate's death. They were with us at almost the very moment we received word of Nate's passing away, and they comforted us. "God's will was for Nate to live a long and healthy life. The enemy of Nate's soul knew that if he could end your son's life, he might be able to end Nate's influence and the influence of the rest of your family for Jesus; therefore, not allowing all of the Mansfields to impact other hurting people's lives with hope. Well, Satan was wrong."

I've learned that my worst fear as a parent is the death of my child. But this fear can be faced, overcome, and used in a mighty way in the lives of my family, others, and myself.

Nate's choice to abuse illegal and prescription drugs and to live in the unhealthy underbelly of life brought about his incarceration, his drug dependency, and so much of his pain. Satan wanted Nate's impact to be nothing. The enemy of Nate's soul was wrong.

Even when Nate was stoned and snowboarding in the mountains of Idaho with friends who also used drugs, God told him to save the life of one of his friends who had accidently snowboarded into dangerous snow on the precipice of a canyon wall. All Nate's others friends, stoned as they were, boarded away, laughing at this young man's plight. At the graveside service, this same young man, one of Nate's pallbearers, broke down while telling the story to all of us. "Without Nate boarding in to help me, then crawling on his belly in the snow to give me his snowboard, I would have died. I was without hope." That was Nate, even when he was high. To his friends his role was of hero/philosopher/party guy— even theological foil.

The struggle within my son was evidenced through his drug abuse, and it was also evidenced

*"The enemy of Nate's soul knew that if he could end your son's life, he might be able to end Nate's influence. Well, Satan was wrong."*

through his occasional willingness to debate his drug friends about God and Jesus. Once when Susan and I were with Nate, he introduced us to an older friend of his—a man about my age. This man lived an addict's life, making a living selling this or that as well as drugs. He had in his possession a series of Civil War–era pocketknives and wanted to sell a couple to my son. While there, Nate somehow got into a theological discussion with this fellow. I was asked to join in. I'll always remember hearing Nate confront this man with the truth about Jesus' life, death, and resurrection. The man listened intently, then sold Nate two small knives and departed. Later, my wife and I compared notes. She asked me if I had also noticed that Nate had made a drug purchase from the man as we were departing. Nate's was a torn life.

## Closing Memories

At Nate's memorial service, his best friends, Andre Alfonso and Mark Smit, joined our family in providing eulogy remarks. Amid tears and fond memories, Mark did in death what he apparently had a hard time doing in Nate's life: he ended the debate on the penny being dropped from the Empire State Building, to the roar of laughter from Nate's friends and family. Unwrapping a sheet of paper he had in his pants pocket, Mark read out loud: "According to Google (which we didn't have when we were in fourth grade), a penny thrown from the top of the Empire State Building wouldn't kill anyone. A penny only weighs about a gram and it tumbles as it falls. Because of the tumbling and the light weight, there's so much air resistance that the penny never really gathers that much speed before it hits its terminal velocity." We needed to laugh, and Mark gave us that chance.

Nate and Colin both played a special role in each other's lives, as did their cousins. One cousin, Kale Rampenthal, put it this way on a recent blog post:

I walked into the funeral parlor room on the right with my mom. There Nate was, dressed in his hoodie. A quilt draped over half of his casket. Flowers were all around; the smell of flowers and death. It's not something you forget. I saw his fiancée crying in the corner, next to his body. She was a total mess. There were more pictures in there. The story of his life, in pictures, was laid out for everyone to see. I walked over and touched his cold dead body. That was the hardest thing to do. I was crying. I was crying hard. It was real. After that harsh realization I went back into the other room, trying to stop the tears. I sat on the couch. My eyes began to dry. As I sat there I watched my aunt and uncle, I watched everyone. I could see so much emotion, so much grief. Enough grief to flood a city. After a while we left. We went to the house owned by my aunt and uncle.

That night my cousin Colin and I drove down to his church youth group in a Corvette owned by my uncle's friend Michael Boerner. (It was nice being able to enjoy something while in such a bad situation.) We blasted the sound system. We would try to take both of our minds off of the pain, by laughing. We were actually laughing a lot, which was a very good thing.

The next day, perhaps the most shocking thing was seeing all of the people who came to his memorial service; too many to count, in fact. We went into the sanctuary to find seats. The stage was in plain view and so was the casket. The smell of flowers filled the entire room with an unforgettable fragrance. The service began, with music playing. The slideshow of my cousin's life in pictures began to play. As the pictures grew closer to the end of his life, the crowd's tears began to flow more intensely. Then the family members began speaking. They told what they remembered. They spoke of the good times, even some spoke of the bad. There was no way a grown man could even control a tear from falling. My throat was swelled up, as I was gasping for air, bawling my eyes out. I was only 14 years old at the time. Through all of this, I learned that tragedy shapes the character, morals define it, and love makes it.

Good words from a very young man.

## What I've Learned

I've learned a lot since Nate's death.

I've learned a few things in my open failures that may be of service to you as you finish this book.

I've learned that I don't have all the answers. In many instances, I don't even have the questions. My past bravado in posing and pretending may have looked good, but it was not good. It was flawed. Admitting that I just simply do not know is both refreshing and honest.

*I've learned that I don't have all the answers. In many instances, I don't even have the questions.*

Many of us primp and position ourselves as if we are something when in reality we are failing; we often go to ridiculous extremes to hide our failures. More than that, many of us live our lives as though we're wearing our parents' clothes, hoping no one challenges us as adults—that no one discovers who we really are.

We sneak into adulthood, feeling as though we're not really adults. We position ourselves within a lie and then go about believing it.

And then, as believers in Christ, we lie to ourselves about believing that what He said is what He meant—especially the parts about loving ourselves and being valuable in God's eyes just as we are.

I often ask people of faith if they love themselves. The common answer I receive from born-again evangelicals ranges between "No, I don't believe we should love ourselves" to "God wants us to love only Him—I really shouldn't love myself." The intensity of the responses is interesting as well. Sometimes the words are laced with deep offense and anger toward me for even asking the question.

My response each time is simple and straightforward: "Quoting Leviticus, Jesus said that you are 'to love your neighbor as yourself.' If you don't love yourself, you cannot love your neighbor." Christians often stand dumbfounded.

There is a prevailing series of unintended lies in evangelical Christianity that have been allowed to take root in the last thirty years. One lie says that loving ourselves is sin. Another says there are secrets to child raising and good marriages—that only some have the secrets and the rest of us should visit their websites and buy their products. The thinking seems to be, "If we follow enough formulas and read enough books, we'll master the to-do list and work harder to gain a balanced and fulfilled life in Christ as parents." Children will follow us, we awkwardly reason, if we push them to do so. If they do not follow us voluntarily, we will make them do so. The default position to discipline becomes an excuse for breaking our children's hearts *and* their spirits.

This same reasoning says that if our lives are in chaos and being ripped apart at the seams, something is internally wrong. "We must make every effort *not* to show the damage," this reasoning quietly states.

I've seen this, because I have lived it. Not only is it disingenuous and wrong, it simply does not work.

I've learned that Nate played a certain role in our family. In that role, he acted irresponsibly and rebelliously. That was the Nate I knew in his later years, but it wasn't the Nate that truly was. His years as an adult and his death had very little to do with us as his parents and family. It was his life, and he chose to live it his way. He initially took drugs, and eventually drugs took him.

I've realized that all children really are on loan to us and that they will all meet Christ face-to-face one day. As I wrote in my first journal entry in Nate's baby book, "You were loaned to us from the Lord." I was correct.

Every child is on loan. And loans have to be repaid. Our children will die and they will stand before the Lord who created them, just as you and I will.

I've learned that I never was my children's police officer. I wasn't their trainer or their life coach. I was not even my children's permanent father, nor are they my permanent little kids. We are brothers and sisters in the Lord.

*I've learned that I never was my children's police officer.*

As parents, we are given many tasks to do; our paramount duty is to love our children in the Lord, and our parallel task is to raise them into adults.

I've learned that I needed to become a student of my children when it was appropriate and to let them graduate to adulthood, as must ultimately be the case. Every set of parents has to decide whether they're going to raise children or adults.

In raising adults, we're passing our children on to God. After all, He's their real father. My desire is for you to be encouraged as you love your kids and raise your beautiful boys and girls to adulthood. There are no secret codes, nor are there any easy 1-2-3 steps. There is just God's love flowing through us to them. I encourage you to love your children and know that God loves them more than you do and that He'll do with them as He pleases. It is up to us to bless the name of the Lord, no matter what.

*The step-by-step formulaic approach to raising children is convenient; it's just invalid.*

As a leader in the conservative Christian community for many years, I eventually saw what worked and what did not. It took the harsh reality of seeing my son's honesty, even when he was high, regarding the false sense of performance-based faith that has plagued evangelical Christianity over these last thirty years. The step-by-step formulaic approach to raising children is convenient; it's just invalid. In an odd way, it could actually be said to achieve its goal: raising children.

But the world doesn't need more children. It needs men and women of integrity who are real, despite the pain and, more important, *because* of the pain. The world is crying out for Jesus, and I have offered them a failed photocopy of Him. Maybe you? The case can be made that the very difficult things that Keith Green and Nate Mansfield presented could only be heard through the megaphone of death. The importance of truth resonates with a dying world—a world full of people who know deep down that there is more to life than what they are living, and yet they do not find it in the Christian evangelical world right now.

But they can, because God brings people to your door and you don't have to. As Keith Green said in his song "Asleep in the Light," just smile and say, "God bless you, be at peace. / And all Heaven just weeps." Nope, you are the one. Rise up and touch the world. Nate did.

As a result of Nate, I also learned something else about my own torn life. I too have been controlled by chemicals—chemicals that kill with as great an intensity as the illegal and prescription pills that affect drug addicts. My drugs, my chemicals may be yours, too. They're the acceptable Christian kind: the consumption of certain foods through a terrible diet. I realized through this experience with Nate how terribly enslaved I had become to a poor diet. I saw a young father of a beautiful baby boy increase by sixty-plus pounds to become a middle-aged hypocrite. Later, I could see the dull eyes and slurred speech of that same son because of his drug behavior, but I ignored my own incredible increase in weight and my demand for sugar and fatty foods. I learned through rejection by neighboring religious people of the staffed, safe, and sober homes that, in fact, I shared in their hypocrisy.

*The evangelical community loves God, yet so many of us treat his temple like a rented room in a rundown motel.*

People don't want recovering substance abusers living near them, yet they'll consume fast food chemicals and self-medicate through drugs in quantities that can cause certain death by heart disease and high blood pressure. I looked in the mirror three years after Nate's death and saw a bloated sugarholic. It terrified me. Some dear friends, Ray and Margaret Robnett, challenged Susan and me to acknowledge our dependency, just as Nate ultimately did, and change our lives through diet. I have done so. My health is returning through enjoying fresh fruit and vegetables and a virtual absence of sugar and other chemicals. My body is healthy. I have lost more than thirty pounds and am continuing to lose more. The evangelical community loves God, yet so many of us treat his temple like a rented room in a rundown motel. I learned from Nate that I would no longer live that way.

## *A True Story*

This has been the true story, from a father's point of view, of a young man's struggle with drug addiction and his eventual death. My hope is that you found it to be full of poignant accounts of the realization that even when, as a parent, you do everything by the book, things often turn out very wrong—and yet things can turn out eternally right.

On that warm and gorgeous first day of spring 2009, Nate was buried in one of the oldest cemeteries in Boise. Nate would have liked that, with his love of history and his appreciation of all the stories that each old grave marker held. Near a U.S. senator and World War II soldiers, my son was laid to rest.

When the service was over, his casket was lowered down into the grave. We stood around the grave as a family, held hands, and sang the nighttime song that, in his childhood, followed every one of our stories about Nathan the Adventurer:

*Jesus loves me when I'm good*
*When I do the things I should.*
*Jesus loves me when I'm bad,*
*Though it makes Him very sad.*
*Yes, Jesus loves me.*
*Yes, Jesus loves me.*

*Yes, Jesus loves me.*
*The Bible tells me so.*

We rejoiced because Nate was not there. He was sitting on one of his sofas in Heaven; Nathan the Adventurer was now on the adventure of his lifetime.

# Part Three

In Loving Memory of Nate

# Nate's Final Pastor

*Nate had three significant pastors help him during his last years of life. Pastor Mark Stewart of Boise took valuable time to visit my son in jail a few key times. His words were kind and his questions were honest. Whenever Nate visited Boise, Mark was always thoughtful enough to meet with him. Without Mark and Jan Stewart, we would never have been able to house and help ex-convicts. Mark "got" Nate. A pastor's heart often understands an inmate's fear. Mark did. Nate met a pastor during the final forty-one days of his life who helped him and yet remains anonymous to us, since he, too, was an inmate. However, most important to Nate's time in jail was Pastor David Snyder of Meridian, Idaho. These are his well-sharpened observations of Nate Mansfield.*

Nate and I met for the first time in jail. He was an inmate and I was a visitor. This particular institution didn't allow face-to-face visits. Glass in between was it. And it was the only way I ever knew Nate.

His parents were my friends, and through them I'd learned of Nate's addiction and ensuing incarceration. Nate, though, was a piece of their life with which I had no experience. When his choices and God's specialized plan of formation landed him in the local jail, I went to see him. Largely, I wanted to bless his parents, Dennis and Susan. And I hoped to speak life to Nate. God let me do both.

As I sat on the stool in the visiting room for the first time, Nate sauntered in. He was disheveled and scruffy, dressed in an orange scrubs-like uniform. Unshaven face, shaven head, and a skin condition exacerbated by life in jail. Expectedly, he was awkward, reserved. We started with the usual pleasantries and polite questions: who I was, how I came to visit him, a bit about my relationship with his parents.

Before my first visit, I decided two things. First, I would go back for a second visit only if he wanted me to, and second, I would go back if I could talk with him about his relationship with Jesus. I asked both questions up front, during the first visit. I wanted to be clear about my intentions. Things got awkward. He didn't seem to include me in many deep elements of his life. It didn't go far that day. Even though he knew I planned on more discussions about Jesus if I returned, he said he wanted to see me again. With that, I left. Over the next few months, I saw him multiple times and began to understand, in a small way, that he lived between two worlds. It was painful to see and painful for him to live.

## Nate the Conservative

"George Bush (the second) wasn't a true conservative. Bill Clinton was a disaster." Television kept him up on politics, and we'd talk about it. He was a political and social conservative. Couldn't help it. Nate read a lot and thought a lot. Conservatism made sense to him. It's what thinking people thought. He wasn't a modern, oxymoronic, economic conservative. He was an abortion-is-wrong, truth-is-objective, morality-is-good, Ronald-Reagan-is-cool conservative.

As we talked about life inside, it was clear Nate didn't think the other inmates cared too much about what mattered to him. He felt it was absurd *not* to think about politics and economics and elections. While he kept to himself in jail for the most part, he did have enough interaction with the other inmates to make some conclusions about them. And himself. He thought about stuff that mattered, and, predominantly, they didn't.

Like many incarcerated people, his perceptions of others and himself weren't grounded. He thought he was different from the others. And, in some ways, he was. In others, he wasn't. Mostly, they deserved to be there, but he wasn't sure he did. He never communicated to me that he'd actually done something wrong. Maybe the other guys had. A languid undercurrent of disbelief trickled through his words, quietly shouting, *Was anybody really hurt by my addiction?*

Authority and authority figures usually come up when I talk to people convicted of crimes. They did with Nate. A deep-rooted paradigm of victimization seeps into their minds. Others act. Convicts are acted upon. Others—parents, cops, judges, girlfriends—did it to them; they didn't do anything to deserve what they got. Connecting behaviors and their natural consequences isn't most inmates' forte. To placate their consciences and excuse their behaviors, their thoughts inform them that someone else was at fault. Nate was suspicious of those who put him in jail. I'm not sure he thought he should be locked up, waiting for his fate to be decided by judges and attorneys. He wasn't sure he'd done anything wrong. Again, maybe the other people did. He was, on the one hand, a thoughtful, conservative, well-reasoned, and intelligent young man. On the other, he was an addict, rejecting the ideals of truth and rightness he espoused. Self-government was at the heart of what seemed right to Nate. People had to be responsible for themselves if a culture was to remain intact and right. But he didn't live this way—and somewhere deep inside I believed that he knew that. He was in two places, both of which were real to him. Both had a claim on him, and he was torn between them.

## Nate, the Son and Brother

I didn't talk much about my family. Nate didn't ask except to be polite. I didn't share for the same reason. I, however, didn't reciprocate his politeness. I invaded. Our conversations progressed, and his confusion and pain began to surface. He never came right out and said, Here's my pain and how it got here. I knew if I watched and listened, I would see it.

He was mad at his dad. He didn't fully understand why his dad did what he did as a Christian, aspiring politician and businessman, or father. Like the sons of many men who choose a deliberate and even controversial direction for their ministry or business endeavors (Dennis was the director of Focus on the Family's Idaho affiliate called Idaho Family Forum), Nate wondered aloud if a plain job might not have been better.

Of course, there was his part to play in his father's choices. As the son of a prominent Christian leader, he was expected to be together, submitted, honoring. Nate didn't like this role. Too much pressure, too many expectations. It was chosen for him without his consent. Dennis's demands were too high. No, they were *wrong;* Nate, of course, was right. I got the distinct impression on more than one occasion that Nate had spent a lot of time thinking about the ways he'd been wronged by his father. I'm not sure he spent the same amount of time pondering the pain he caused his father and mother.

*I got the distinct impression on more than one occasion that Nate had spent a lot of time thinking about the ways he'd been wronged by his father.*

He thought his mom's view of Dennis was not accurate, resenting the fact that she, at times, worked full-time to support his father's unsuccessful business and political ambitions. Dennis should have done a better job supporting the family. Susan shouldn't have covered for him. She could've done something else. Probably things would have been different. Dennis didn't quite get the provider thing right. This might not have been obvious to his mom or the rest of the world, but it was to Nate.

Confusion set in. His struggle with his father overflowed into subtle misperceptions of his place in the family. Moms have to work out their issues with dads. No other way to marital reconciliation. It can't be done for them. If sons champion the grievances they believe and want their mothers to have, expectations of everyone else and themselves get warped. Landing in the middle of relational dynamics that weren't his, he couldn't resolve them. In his own heart, he was between the two people he loved most. It's an impossible place for sons to live. Nate was there and it wasn't working.

Meg, Nate's sister, mostly agreed with him about their parents and father—or so he thought—but he conceded she worked her issues out differently. Her methods were more constructive than his. Somehow, she grabbed the independence they both craved and was able, at the same time, to say what she wanted to say. When Meg came up in conversation, it felt to me like Nate didn't understand what he thought he did about her. He presumed certain things, then assumed Meg's perceptions matched. On the other hand, it also seemed like he knew something existed between Meg and Dennis he couldn't quite explain. How could she see what he saw about her dad and yet engage in a meaningful relationship with him? It was an inexplicable dichotomy to Nate.

Nate loved Colin, his younger brother. Affection silently percolated in him when Colin came up in conversation. While his fondness for Colin was passive, it was so real it penetrated me and left me with affection for Colin I didn't previously experience.

During my visits with Nate, he clearly thought Colin was young and didn't yet realize he might be wound too tight, like Nate was. Too many demands, relational and religious. Colin would probably blow out, like he did. As best as I could tell, he didn't want Colin to follow in his footsteps. He loved his brother. When he said he didn't want Colin to blow out, I believed him, but what he said didn't sit right with me.

When Nate referred to his own background, he didn't give much away. What he said was vague, elusive. Something was missing, and I think it was remorse. And, without remorse, his eyes and expectations weren't clear—about his brother, his father, and himself.

Nate didn't want to deal with what was between him and his father. I asked. Maybe he didn't want to talk about it through the glass. Maybe it was because I had no place in his life. Either way, there was something else. Since he had not yet come to terms with his own failings and sins, I think part of him would have felt vindicated if Colin fell. In a twisted sort of way, it seemed like he thought it might help his dad see how he'd failed Nate. And he desperately wanted his dad to realize how wrong he was.

Two worlds swirled inside him. One called for repentance; the other harbored resentment. He was between truth and deception, calling for his dad's confession and repentance while at the same time refusing to do the same. What he insisted on from others, he refused to give. He was trapped, blinded by what he thought others owed him.

Personal repentance and remorse is the only remedy for the misery inflicted on us by resentment. Nate didn't know that no amount of penance from his dad would resolve his confusion.

On the one hand, he hated what he perceived his dad wanted from him, and on the other, he desperately wanted his father to satiate his brokenness with impossible measures of contrition. This was the tragedy of his relationships. What he expected, he wouldn't give. With him living between these two conflicting demands, his relationships were unmanageable.

## Nate, the Christian

As I listened to Nate over the course of our visits, I didn't get a lot of direct information about his Christianity. There was some. Much of what I derived about Nate's relationship with Jesus was ascertained from what I knew of his relationships with others. The Apostle John tells us interpersonal relationships are a reliable source of information about one's bond with Him (1 John 4:7–11). They certainly were for Nate. Between our discussions about people and politics and Jesus, Nate's Christianity showed up.

I asked him if he thought he was a Christian and implied

strongly that he should consider the question. I suggested he might not be. "Don't assume you are a Christian just because you were raised in a Christian home or said the sinner's prayer," I told him. I started from the beginning with the Gospel. I didn't tell him I was; I just did. "The consuming hunger in you cannot be quenched with anything besides Jesus' life." What drugs and rebellion did *for* him was minuscule in comparison to what Jesus would do *in* him. I talked about the blood of Jesus, that trust means surrender, and that surrender is earthy, practical, tangible. It can't remain in the world of ideas and images. Relationships, actions, attitudes change in us when we repent. Escapism wasn't the answer. A brutal encounter with reality in the person of Jesus was.

I never had a doubt Jesus was intertwined with Nate's life. His face, his words, and his paradigms betrayed him. The Messiah had thrown an anchor into his life, and it was wedged in the secret places of his heart. In spite of the shortfalls that may have been present in his family and church experience, Jesus got into Nate. But, for Nate, it seemed Jesus was obscured by Nate's unrelenting passions for what was inherently incompatible with Heaven.

My hope as I visited Nate was to kindle what the Spirit and his parents' love and faithfulness had planted in him. I didn't tell him anything he hadn't heard before. His parents are godly. They know and love Jesus. They're faithful. Rather than shrivel into bitter resentment, they used Nate's addiction as a springboard for life-changing ministry to addicts. I was part of it. It was amazing. And, since his death, they have pressed on to joy, ministering life to my family and me in the midst of their own loss. So, I speak as a beneficiary of their faithfulness.

As a result, I am sure that in the midst of all their parental failings, they spoke and imparted Jesus' life to Nate. Kingdom seeds lived in the soil of his heart. Maybe the ground was fallow, maybe rocky. One way or the other, Jesus was part of Nate's growing up. And part of him.

Both the difficulty and blessing of Jesus is that He is a faithful shepherd. Abandonment isn't part of His DNA. So His dogged fidelity was really inconvenient for Nate. His addiction was a boisterous cry that he wanted to be left alone. But because Jesus' life had been deposited in him in such a substantial way, it was also a longing cry that said he *couldn't* be left alone. Jesus wanted his entire life. Nate wanted to give it to Him, and he wanted to keep it, too. The inevitable collision was a morass of guilt alleviation and conflicted affirmation, passivity and reaction, rejection and rejecting, elation and misery, grace and performance.

What was problematic for Nate, and is for all of us, is that God's grace and mercy are violent, devastating when they invade. Mercy says we're frantic and miserable in poverty but also says God's life is the exclusive source of riches. Grace says we're wholly insufficient for our own redemption but also says God is capable of rescuing us and willing to do it. Like many in Nate's position, he found his life interrupted by the offer of grace and mercy, which wrecked what he hoped to build outside the confines of His Kingdom. Frankly, Jesus just messed with his plans. Forget the physical and psychological addiction to drugs, as real as they are. The *spiritual* addiction they create always ends in a heaping pileup with God's agenda. And there's only one Kingdom that stands in the end. Nate couldn't have both.

Like a lot of people raised by faithful, believing parents, Nate wanted the world. Lived in it. Loved it. Never once, though, did it give him the life he tasted in Jesus. Cognitively, he knew drugs wouldn't give him anything lasting. In his heart, though, delusion was so deeply embed-  *Jesus' dogged fidelity was really inconvenient for Nate.*

ded he tried and tried to wrest life from death. What his mind knew was true waged war with what his soul believed it needed. Distanced from Jesus' life and presence, he was never content in the world. Even with all its lures and baubles, it just wasn't enough. If eyes could see past the veneer of his rebellion, Nate was ruined for the world.

And like many of those same people raised by faithful, believing parents, he wanted Jesus. The problem, really, was that Nate couldn't *escape* Jesus. He was an unshakable fixture in his life. He tried to live in the world, but Jesus was there, breaking in with broken relationships, arrests, jail, judges, and financial turmoil, ruining perfectly good plans. At first glance, the solution seems easy: choose the world and let Jesus go. Heaven was real for Nate, though, and he never seemed able to ignore it for long.

Many who are raised in believing homes and churches end up their most ardent accusers. Some reject God altogether. Some don't go this far. Instead, they reject, to one degree or another, the responsibility and implications of His existence. And many end up going to the grave enveloped in this lie. Somewhere along the way, in the perennial cycle of difficult relationships and painful events, they become convinced God hasn't been good to them. Then, with growing accusation, they set out to find goodness on their own. It's drugs for some, marriage and children for others. For all practical purposes, God is the source of their misery, and getting away from Him is the perceived solution.

No matter how the specifics play out, what ends up happening is that they try to detach themselves from the reality of God's existence and involvement. Their assumption is pretty straightforward: *If I reject God and live as if He doesn't exist and isn't involved, then I can secure my own good.* In the end, they leave, spiritually, relationally, emotionally, or physically. And it never works.

This violates one of the foundational principles of God's Kingdom: sowing and reaping. Humans can't sow seeds of accusation and rebellion, walk away from God, and then receive life. Disconnection and life are mutually exclusive.

When they leave, death keeps collecting in and around them, starts occupying more space, and eventually consumes them. Shocked and angry, accusations intensify. God is on the firing line, and for good measure, Christian families and churches are usually thrown in. But the fallacy is obvious: if God doesn't exist or isn't involved, how can He be held responsible for the fruit they do or do not harvest? If they've set out to secure their own good and are convinced they can, why bring God into the picture again? What is missed in the mire of lies is that God *has been faithful* in keeping His Word. When we live as if He doesn't exist and isn't involved, death naturally follows. He told us this in advance so there would be no confusion (Galatians 6:7–8). Consequences are one of the strongest evidences that He can be trusted.

Nate wanted to live as he chose. Do what he wanted to do. Be what he wanted to be. And he wanted Jesus' eternal, abundant life at the same time. All his efforts to change the spiritual dynamics of the universe were ludicrous. He just didn't know it. Gravity doesn't change for the ignorant, ill informed, or rebellious. Neither does sowing and reaping. Nate lived in constant conflict because he couldn't find life in addiction. The universe wouldn't change for him, and so he had to eat the fruit of his choices.

God's faithfulness was displayed in every judge, in jail and prison, in broken relationships, in the financial hardship, in the mistrust with his parents and estrangement from his family. These were proof that God kept His Word, but Nate couldn't see it. I remember emphatically telling him. Jesus narrowed Nate's life and brought him face to face with His loving intention to disciple him.

It just happened to be that the discipleship necessary at that point in his life was through the justice system. My words were met with incredulity.

Nate invested in death, demanded life, and when death's fruit was all that was left, he descended into a chasm of accusation. Jesus couldn't be trusted because he was in jail, because relationships in his life were strained and broken, because drugs didn't satisfy. The list was long but not always detailed, at least not to me. However, I was left with the impression that details were readily available to him, which was part of his struggle. When accusation takes hold, there's no end to the distortions we can forge, the worst of which is this: we can secure life by blaming others for its absence in us.

*Nate invested in death, demanded life, and when death's fruit was all that was left, he descended into a chasm of accusation.*

In all the time I spent with Nate, he never made a convincing confession that he was a believer. Neither did he deny it. The issue just hung out there in the space between us. When he did speak of Jesus, it was with strained distance, an awkward reality motivating him in ways he could not explain. Jesus seemed a quandary for Nate. Spiritually, he was muddled. Practically, he was an addict. He was between the worlds of life and death and they don't coexist for very long in any of us. Either we will hate one and love the other, or we will love one and despise the other. Nate was stuck between his desire for life and death.

## Nate, the Prophet

Evangelical Christianity was part of Nate. Not part of his experience—it was part of him. Christian politics and worldview, church on Sunday and all that comes with it, parachurch ministries, conferences, traveling to do missions work, and meeting prominent Christian leaders was in the mixing bowl for him. "Faith, Family, and Freedom" was a familiar mantra. He was the proverbial insider. Knew the stuff, knew the people, knew the assets and liabilities. He lived them. They became part of him.

When I say evangelical Christianity was part of Nate, I don't mean he loved it or necessarily wanted to be part of it. At least, not in obvious ways or for obvious reasons. In his mind, he was outside. He wasn't a purveyor of most of its stated tenets, wasn't dedicated to promoting it, and was reluctant to identify with it. His lifestyle, in large measure, clashed with it. He knew it and knew other Christians did as well. Here, I began to see another component of Nate's life.

While he didn't give me a lot of specific information, in many ways church was wreckage for him. A submerged *them and me* attitude came up when we talked about it. Church seemed like an extension of the pain and disappointment he faced with his father. And with Jesus. If he was strained with them, how could it not be with church?

From conversations I've since had with his parents, they came to realize Nate wanted to experience love in ways others misunderstood. His temperament and personality were outside the norm. As a boy, Nate was rambunctious, energetic, curious, intelligent, and even irritating. Traits like these don't usually bode well for a boy in a middling church. In fact, the two of them are on a crash course.

The relationship is often forced, and more often than not, the boy must conform to standards that don't make sense to him (though I'm not sure all of them *should* make sense).

Right or wrong, Nate felt ostracized, rejected, an outsider with no way in. To cross the threshold into acceptance, he'd have to surrender. And he wouldn't.

As I prayed for him during my visits, I asked myself, *What made surrender so repulsive?* Combining what I learned from Nate and his parents, I ascertained he was in the agonizing position of embracing ideas and experiences for which there was, or at least appeared to be, contradiction and hypocrisy.

In part, his reluctance was valid. Evangelicalism sometimes asks for surrender in ways that inadvertently produce death. It's not that there's some intentional evangelical conspiracy at work, sending infiltrators to church foyers and pulpits to kill life. However, there are aspects that exalt knowledge above life, intellect above love, the ink and paper of the Bible above the Living Word, works above grace. And when Nate came along, he wouldn't give in to what he knew was death. But he also wouldn't surrender to the life that *was* there. It was a package deal for Nate. He didn't want to become hypocritical and rejecting, like the people in church who misunderstood and wounded him. So he rejected much of what he'd seen and known in church and many of the people along the way.

In the end, he did become like them. What we focus on, we become. Nate allowed his experiences to morph into a critical, judgmental spirit and, in all the time I knew him, it remained there. Once a critical spirit takes hold, we're attached to those who actually have, or we think have, offended us. He was hooked and didn't know it. The hypocrisy and rejection he despised swallowed him up.

He sat in judgment of the other inmates, of his father and family, of Jesus, and of the church. While he projected that he didn't want to be inside, it wasn't true. His

*He was hooked and didn't know it. The hypocrisy and rejection he despised swallowed him up.*

judgmental spirit betrayed him. A critical, offended spirit is always looking for something—something we perceive was withheld or something taken that shouldn't have been. And we're looking for restitution of that something from the person or persons who hurt us. Nate was looking for something from church, something he thought he didn't get or should have gotten. It was as if there were a magnet drawing him to engage the culture he thought had so rejected him.

So when I say evangelical Christianity was part of Nate, the elements of it that are contradictory and hurtful did become part of him. His character reflected the core weaknesses of Christians today. He hated it but it soaked into his heart.

Honestly, more goodness and righteousness soaked into his heart than what he might have been willing to admit. The spiritual saturation he received in church and family life did, in part, take root. When Nate looked at his life in light of what he'd grown up in, he had to face what he *wasn't*. An inner mirror was ever before him, reflecting the fact that the way he lived wasn't right. Where did his conviction come from? Social constructs? Cultural norms? No, they came from Christianity. It was part of him.

I believe Christianity was part of Nate for another reason, too. He did want to be restored to relationships with his family, with Jesus, and with the body of Christ. I don't mean "restored" in the sense of a shallow, cultural acceptance that trifles with life and truth. No, part of him clung to Heaven's reality and to mercy and righteousness. Something in him knew Jesus was beautiful and the church valuable.

I sat across from him one day in the visiting room and said with urgency, "Nate, you're a prophet to the body of Christ." Something in him, buried in rebellion and addiction, hungered for significance and purpose. Somewhere, I sensed his life was destined to bring prophetic insight, truth, and correction to Jesus' people. He judged the church and saw weakness and pride and inconsistency in it. He was too smart and discerning not to see these things. He ran away, but his spiritual sight never left him.

He was a prophet—he just didn't know it. Rebellion was, in many ways, a safe haven for Nate, but something about it didn't fit him. Burnings in prophets don't go away just because they're broken, critical people. They get tilted and slanted, hazy and selfish. But they don't leave.

Nate had a prophetic call on his life. But it had to be surrendered to Jesus, to spiritual authority, and to the church before it could be released and cultivated. Making good on his deposit, God kept confronting him with truth. The Father was trying to bring Nate to his knees through judges, jail and prison, spiritual authority, and opportunities for freedom. And every time he had to choose.

*Rebellion was . . . a safe haven for Nate, but something about it didn't fit him.*

In one of our last visits, I told Nate that God was trying to break his heart. He wanted to remove the bitter arrogance in him so he could speak life to His church. Prophets who speak before they're broken by God's mercy are scathing and harsh. God was preparing Nate to speak with compassion and grace, from his own surrender and victory, from a life interwoven with God's heart.

Multiple opportunities came to Nate so he could submit to

God's breaking. I wasn't in his life when he passed away because the beast of addiction still held him. The breaking wasn't complete. He was between the familiar zone of addiction, and everything that went along with it, and God's prophetic call on his life. I am sure it was painful for Nate. And I am sure it was even more painful for God.

## Nate, the Teacher

Nate didn't visibly encounter Jesus during my visits. We'd talk, I'd exhort, he'd listen and maybe ask a few questions, and then I'd leave. I wanted to speak life to Nate, and Jesus let me do that. For this reason alone, my time was fruitful. Nate was transferred to the prison system in Missouri shortly after our last visit. After he was released, he came back to Boise for a short time. Through his parents, I let him know I wanted to see him. But we never met. He didn't seem to have the time or interest. Then, after another incarceration and release, he passed. It was awful.

Nate left some things with me, though.

He was a convoluted, confused jungle of conviction and compromise, clarity and confusion, truth and condemnation, desire and apathy. His in-between-ness was conspicuous, on the table to see if someone cared to look long and hard enough. So it's important to ask, *What does Nate have to say to us?* There are many still alive in this generation in between Heaven and Hell, like Nate was. We can learn something from Nate for their sake.

Because he was in between, an insider and outsider, Nate spoke with a voice that was at once judgmental *and* true. So, should we listen to him? Truth is a rare commodity in our culture, even in the church. In an age of easy believe-ism and pain-free Christianity, Nate didn't mind saying what many others don't want to say or, more important, hear. Are all his words true? No! But I hope we're ready to listen to the true parts of what he had to say. Brash and brazen words and actions come from people who've walked Nate's road. And where their pain and sorrow intersects with truth, we're often on the receiving end of some profound insights.

The criticisms of Nate's generation are more valid than we'd like to think, but not for the reasons that *they* think. If we look beyond his words, we can hear what Nate's life said. His words were important, but they were unstable, cynical, and occasionally punitive. What I believe is of greatest value was what he said with his life.

*Where their pain and sorrow intersects with truth, we're often on the receiving end of some profound insights.*

In part, Nate reacted to a strained, distant evangelical-ism that speaks of truth and intellectualism as synonyms. They're not. Truth is not a series of propositional statements we are supposed to teach our children so they can acquire the right doctrines and a biblical worldview. When truth is presented as a set of defined presuppositions to be memorized, quoted, and used to defend the faith, we miss the point altogether.

And herein lies the dilemma: Nate knew truth in the propositional sense. His experience with truth as a daily transforming reality was incomplete, though. In so many ways, Jesus was ideas and images, not experiential truth and salvation.

On this point, the Christian culture of today is greatly influenced by the world's culture. "The end of knowledge is power," said Thomas Hobbes. He was wrong, but we've imbibed and now we're tipsy with it. Getting more knowledge about the Bible or

God or any other subject is not, in and of itself, transforming. Yes, we worship God with our minds, but we also worship Him with our souls, our spirits, our strength, and, most important, our hearts. For this in-between generation, Christian knowledge and morality is insufficient. They are not looking for concepts of truth. They are looking for truth in the person of Jesus, which we cannot have without the experiential truth of His presence and power transforming our lives.

Are doctrine and knowledge important? Of course! Can we have an accurate Jesus without objective truth statements? Of course not. I am not saying truth is less than these, but I am saying it's a lot more. Jesus didn't come to defend truth. He *was* truth; it's contained within and flows from Him (John 14:6). When we know Him, we know truth and walk in freedom (John 8:31–32).

Drug addiction was Nate's bondage. Many in-betweens are not addicts, in this sense. Clearly defined morality and doctrine, though, won't keep them from idolatrous marriages, the ravages of divorce, greed and covetousness, consuming anger, and a litany of other miseries. Morally responsible children and families aren't the goal. Transformed disciples are. And where we confuse truth and life with knowledge and intellectualism, we guarantee our own failure.

*Morally responsible children and families aren't the goal. Transformed disciples are.*

Victimization is an institution in our culture. Nate perceived himself, in many ways, as a victim of others' failures. He acted like it, refusing to accept responsibility for much of the havoc he created by his selfish rebellion. His life tells us something about this in-between generation and, to bring life to them, we must substantively address the pervasive victimization under which they toil.

Nate grew up in an imperfect home. All of us did. God gave him to Dennis and Susan without asking his permission, and it came along with all their sin and frailty and brokenness. Were things in the Mansfield household bad? Is that why Nate blew out? In one sense, we could say that much of what happened to Nate wasn't his fault at all, for who of us ends up where we are completely of our own choosing? We didn't choose our parents and their faults; we don't choose what happens to us in the early years of life. We're carried along in life's boat without an oar. Sometimes the waves around our boat are more or less violent than those around another's. Either way, we had little to nothing to do with it.

But let's look at this from a different vantage point: How many men and women Nate's age would have *loved* to be raised in his home, by his parents? If Nate thought his parents were so clouded and unreasonable, how many others would have found life in their home? And how can we explain Nate's younger sister and brother, who faithfully walk with Jesus? Same parents, same household. How can we place blame for Nate's struggles on Dennis and Susan when so many others have received so much life through them?

On a broader scope, we also have to ask, *Who hasn't been victimized?* Or think of it this way: *Who doesn't have reason to accuse God and others?* Bad things happen to everyone. All parents err. Are some situations worse than others? Obviously. Are some more heinous or devastating? Yes. And where the victimization is authentically more devastating, increased patience and compassion are in order.

That, however, is not the point. The point is that because Nate fell prey to the victim mentality, he got stuck in a rut. For a number of years, his family was tormented by his addiction. When I talked to Nate, he had little remorse for what he had done to them. Did he feel bad? Probably. But sorrowful feelings do not equate with remorse and repentance, neither of which seemed present in him. He was very aware of what he thought his family did or didn't do for him, how they failed him, what they should have done differently. In the end, the tables were turned and Nate became the victim.

And it's on this point that we must listen to the lessons of Nate's life. This in-between generation is inundated with messages of victimization, and where victimization is rampant, accusation and entitlement soon follow. We are in the midst of young men and women deeply influenced by the lie *Someone did it to me and now they owe me.* Until we address and correct this lie, we will forever be debtors to them.

On Judgment Day, Jesus will not excuse away anyone's rebellion, anyone rejecting Him, or anyone refusing to serve Him because someone failed them. The culture of victimization and entitlement leads us falsely to believe this is true.

On the surface, it's compelling: *My dad said he was a Christian but rejected me so I rejected Jesus.* Stands to reason, right? Only there's nothing in the Bible to condone a person's rebellion and refusal to serve Jesus because he was rejected or abused. We'll all stand before the Judgment seat of Jesus, and He will ask us what we did or did not do to pursue a relationship with Him.

And from the look of things, no one will be excused for rejecting Jesus for any reason.

Now this is not just an issue of individual significance. In the last thirty years, we've gone from churches that specialize in appealing to Christian consumers to churches that are trying to reach those who were alienated *because* they were treated like consumers. We're trying to do

*Where victimization is rampant, accusation and entitlement soon follow.*

church a whole new way today, building churches to reach those who have been alienated. But, alienated from what and in what way? By compromised churches? By spiritually manipulative parents? By pastors or school principals who failed in their duties by abusing power or sex or money? None of these will be accepted as valid reasons for rejecting Jesus.

For this generation, Nate's a wake-up call. We are prone to think that by sympathizing with and affirming victims in their victimhood, we minister life to them. It's not true. We minister life by calling them into truth and forgiveness, to humility and unity. Life comes when they refuse to play the role of entitled victim and surrender to God's transforming grace. If we don't acknowledge and address this properly, we can actually embolden people to become victims without even knowing it.

In Nate's case, Dennis and Susan acknowledged and turned from much in their lives that was hurtful and damaging to him. They made mistakes, grew through them, and moved on. They walked out of bondage into the richness of God's freedom. In Nate's older years, he received an increasing measure of blessing through his parents as they progressed in love and humility. Still, his response was limited at best. What he said he wanted them to be, they became, and he still wouldn't or couldn't receive it. So he remained the victim.

Dennis and Susan fought hard for life after Nate's death. It didn't have to be that way. They could have succumbed to the lies of victimization and entitlement, falling into the awful place in between. After all, they prayed for Nate for a long time. Dennis started a jail ministry and drug and alcohol rehab precisely because of his experiences with Nate. It wasn't supposed to end this way.

Nate was supposed to come home as the prodigal son, repentant, ready to reconcile.

After he passed, they had the choice to fall into the in-between, like their son. They could have railed at God because of all they gave to Nate, for all the unanswered prayers, for all the unfulfilled promises. There was much that could have been that wasn't because Nate died. They had all the reasons to blame God. But in the wake of Nate's passing, they did exactly what they modeled and taught Nate to do: they held on to Jesus. And just a little over two years after Nate's death, Dennis told me he was starting to feel joy again.

Pastor David Snyder  
268church.org  
Meridian, Idaho

# A Note from Nate's Fiancée

I received an unexpected letter from Nate's fiancée, Ginger Bridger, three months after Nate died. We were feeling the pain of all that we would not experience with our son, and Ginny's letter brought us back to the good things that had happened in her life because of Nate's upbringing. With her permission, I am placing it here for you to see.

*Dennis,*

*I hope you enjoy the movie I am sending with this letter. Nate loved* Big Fish. *He would always get emotional at the end of it because it reminded him of how much he loved you. He was so proud of you, within minutes of first meeting him, I already knew your name and background. He asked me to look you up online; he wanted everyone to know that Dennis Mansfield is his dad. I remember when I did look you up what I found was not based on politics or Nate's troubles but an article you wrote on marriage; I remember because we made sure to apply those principles in our relationship—keeping our relationship Christ-centered, not letting outside failures affect inside success, and belonging to each other.*

*I want to thank you for raising a son who was a big enough man to live under those principles. I also want to thank you for all the other wonderful qualities Nate acquired from you. He is romantic; if we had extra money he would choose an intimate dinner above everything else. He never hid his feelings and would profess his love daily. You taught him to think, he is smart, he can speak to anyone of any age or background. I loved talking to him, we could talk about everything, he is so smart, it was such a blessing to have someone who can sit and discuss the mundane to the political. Although our opinions would differ sometimes, we always had great talks. He had such a sweet, gentle nature. He was kind and compassionate without compromising his manliness. He loved animals, babies, people on the street, his dogs, but mostly he loved his family. He was proud of things other men would have had a hard time expressing their feelings on.*

*He held my hand everywhere we went and always had a hug, he fulfilled my love language, physical touch, while we spent quality time together (Nate's love language).*

*He introduced terms and concepts that have been so hard for me my whole life: apologize and forgiveness.*

*By being that sweet wonderful man you taught him to be, his unconditional love, ability to fix and apologize for his mistakes, [he] eventually rid me of my stubborn will and anger. He was a peacemaker, wanting both him and me to have peace and forgiveness in all our relationships.*

*I think I am most thankful for the love of Christ you and Susan taught him. He made his faith known immediately. He never waffled about his belief and made sure everyone knew what side he was on. I loved watching Nate defend his faith after someone doubted God or the truth. You could just see all his great qualities come out as he spoke—his passion, love, intelligence. He made me so proud. Again, I want to thank you for blessing me with such a wonderful person. I hope your Father's Day is all you deserve.*

*Love,*

*Ginger*

# Nathan Dennis Mansfield, 1981–2009

*Nate Mansfield, twenty-seven, entered into the arms of his personal Savior, Jesus Christ, on Wednesday, March 11, 2009. He passed away in his sleep of accidental causes in his home in Kansas City, Missouri.*

*Nathan Dennis Mansfield was born July 14th, 1981, in Fontana, California, to Dennis and Susan Mansfield.*

*As the firstborn, his was a lifetime of sports, film, politics, and fun. His love of sports began with his first spoken word: "basketball" (no kidding). His love of film began in a baby carrier at the theater:* Raiders of the Lost Ark.

*His love of politics began in a backpack for a 1982 U.S. Congressional race.*

*His love of family was expressed with tender hugs, cackling laughter, and teasing . . . oh, the teasing.*

*When he was three, he welcomed his baby sister, Meg, with a kiss on her head, at the hospital. Later, he welcomed his baby brother, Colin, by taking him to his Christian elementary school for his own fourth-grade show-and-tell, four hours after he was birthed (again, no kidding). His best friend from that time, through high school till now, Mark Smit, was like his brother. They are forever friends. Nate graduated from Boise's Capital High in 2000.*

*As a child he loved spoken stories and would listen intently for hours about "Nathan the Adventurer." He was an auditory learner. As a homeschooler in the initial years, he looked adults in the eye and spoke freely. As a private- and public-schooler he debated his teachers, fellow students, and stood his ground. He was pro-life, conservative, and loved to debate.*

*He played life hard: sports, politics, learning, and love.*

*Named after King David's prophet, Nathan, Nate was fearless with fairness. He wanted things fair. He radiated loyalty and expected it in return. His love language was "quality time" and he passionately loved people; Nate was an evangelist of people. He loved to hear their life stories.*

*No person was a stranger, if they were real with him. He cherished relationships . . . with God and others. He accepted Christ as his Savior when he was young and grew to true manhood, struggling, though, to often consistently live out his faith.*

*Nate spoke with his dad on the phone about Jesus . . . only forty-eight hours before he met the Lord, face-to-face.*

*Nate passionately loved his fiancée, Ginny. He tried to include Christ in their relationship, and they prayed together. She believed in Nate and will carry his memory with her through her life. She loved him deeply. Nate's love of his dogs, Satchel and Clarice, was well known by us and returned to him by them.*

*His struggle with drugs robbed him of years of life. But,*

*death, where is your sting? Grave, where is your victory? Not
with Nate Mansfield, for he is alive in Christ, free at last.*

> *Frost gives way to florid spring,*
> *The norm gets changed, what's happening?*
> *The flowers bloom, the ice recedes,*
> *The trees grow green, as do the leaves,*
> *And so life changes, as it must,*
> *Time moves on, turns to dust,*
> *"Is" becomes "was," present to past,*
> *Like scents in the wind, it happens so fast,*
> *Nate, you're alive, of this we are sure,*
> *You're hangin' with Papa, for death He's the cure.*
> *(by Colin Mansfield, age sixteen)*

*Nate's past is finished. His present is upon him. Your future
with him (or any of those you love) requires your decision for
Jesus.*

*Nate was dearly loved and will be greatly missed by his
parents, Dennis and Susan Mansfield, his sister and brother-in-
law, Meg and Caleb Roe, Nate's nephew, Cole Roe, and Nate's
brother, Colin Mansfield.*

# Sending a Sofa On Ahead

By Dennis Mansfield

March 20, 2009

Good morning. Thank you for honoring Nate today.

Susan, Meg, Caleb, Colin, and I are grateful, as is Ginny.

In this part of the program, I get to tell his story from the perspective that only his dad could deliver. As our friend Chad Estes recently phrased it, Nate Mansfield was an evangelist of other people's lives. He really was.

He loved films and the tales movies told. He was a searcher of other people's stories, listening intently to them, only selectively sharing his own personal stories, struggles, and successes with others—he spoke little of himself and wanted even less about himself in print or on TV. Nate was a sports nut, a political fan, and an accidental change-agent.

And this is my story about him. I'm calling it "Sending a Sofa On Ahead." Hmmm . . . you'll get it.

After I greeted Nate for the first time—at his birth—and saw that mommy and baby were fine, I tiredly left the hospital and fell exhausted into my car. As I turned the ignition key, the radio also came on, and the opening lines of Harry Chapin's "Cat's in the Cradle" met me.

And I wept.

I wept for what I didn't want to happen in his life and in our lives together. In tears, I drove the four or so minutes to my house, sobbing as the song continued.

It was at that point that I determined to live my life as a purposeful father for Nate (and any other kids that could—and did—come along), to *not* be swept away by my career and the foolish things that so tend to occupy our precious minutes on this earth.

Looking in advance to years not possibly known nor even yet expected, I vowed that the concluding words of that song would definitely *not* apply to either Nate's life or mine, should we be blessed to both advance in age.

Just six weeks ago in Kansas City, Nate and I had our last time together. It was an accidental visit, of sorts—planned by God, unplanned by Nate or me.

I was traveling.

A connecting flight was missed; I was rerouted to Kansas City Airport. I called Nate and at midnight, he immediately picked me up at the airport and (since Nate *loved* films), we were off on *Nate and Den's Most Excellent Adventure.*

Back to his childhood.

As Nater grew, his birthdays gave us reasons to celebrate life out loud. Sue and I were California kids with a California baby.

All things were new and we loved life with the VanderWendes and the Switzers, the Raynauds and the Rampenthals, the Woods and the Gozdecks—with our ten siblings, Kathy, Gary, Janet, JoAnne, Joyce, and Ken on my side and Debby, JoAnn, Larry, and Cathy on Susan's side, and many cousins and friends. We built small businesses, and we even built a church.

One day at that church in San Bernardino, a six-year-old version of Nate looked at me, paused, and then dramatically told me: "Dad, I'm gonna send a sofa on ahead."

Puzzled, I asked what he meant.

He said, "Daddy, the Bible says we have mansions in Heaven and that Jesus went ahead to make 'em ready for us. So (he continued) whenever we show love in Jesus' name, it's like we send a sofa on ahead—you know, to fix up our mansion, one thing at a time, for when we get there."

I couldn't argue with his theology. And we began sending sofas on ahead—supporting people in need, mentoring families, giving from our hearts, purposefully living our lives out loud. Nate initiated it.

Where most families' calendars align on the first of January each year, the now-famous birthday parties of Nate—and then Meg and then Colin—seemed to inadvertently identify the *real* start of each new year for us.

And with each year, new adventures unfolded.

Campus by the Sea on Catalina Island was his family favorite, he often told me. CBS, as it is called, is a Christ-centered family camp that was Nate's anchor of consistency, for it has continued to be a priority to annually camp there for over two decades.

Nate reached the full stature of his young manhood under the palm trees and in the sound of surf splashing against the rocks of that island's shoreline, learning about Christ and helping people grow in life. Sending sofas on ahead.

On one of our other adventures, we visited Boise, Idaho, and I knew, somehow, by God's whisper, that we were to move here. So, in time, California became Idaho to Nate. Home became Boise and birthdays eventually gave us candles arranged in teen digits.

Mission trips also occurred. We joined the teenage version of Nate as he played soccer in Europe for a Christian outreach club called the Charlotte Eagles.

As a family, we traveled to Scandinavia to support Nate as he played soccer during the day, and then had him join us as we ministered at night or on unscheduled days of play to the street people, drug addicts, and prostitutes of Gothenburg, Sweden. It wasn't a perfect time, but we did it as a family and we continued sending sofas on ahead.

On that trip, Nate visited Denmark, the Netherlands, Germany, France, and England. He walked the city streets of Hilerød, Amsterdam, Heidelberg, Freiberg, Paris, and London—and he was only sixteen years old.

Nate's adolescence continued to unfold, and the typical "tearing apart" for independence's sake seemed to naturally and painfully occur. It was the semi-open door to adulthood, standing slightly ajar. And Nate seemed uberanxious to move toward that door and ultimately through it.

Nate was fearless with fairness. And teen years are often just not fair. As a family we've had certain sayings that were not quite proverbs, but we kinda felt they should have been. "Life's not fair," we would tell Nate. "Food tastes better when you share it." "Let's pray before we go on vacation," and on and on—small sayings that stay with a family.

Politics happened for Nate. He worked on several campaigns as a teen; some of the legislators he helped now hold high office, and they remember Nate.

But believe it or not, Nate was a shy boy. He hated our family's visibility in the community, hated what he felt were the attacks on his dad in the media, hated the sycophantic nods to us by hangers-on because we were a part of Focus on the Family, hated going to restaurants and having our time as a family interrupted by someone of questionable intentions approaching the table to talk politics.

He loved Woody Wood, Henri Raynaud, and Stewart McLauren in his early years. He loved Michael Boerner, Bill Proctor, and Russ Fulcher in his Idaho years. All were the most significant adult men of his life.

He adored his aunts and uncles—all ten of them. Loved all of his grandparents, including his beloved Mutti—my mother.

But he worshipped his grandpa, my dad—Bill Mansfield. Theirs was a strangely understood and mutually appreciated relationship. An odd couple of like minds and spirits. I wear both their rings on my finger as a reminder of their friendship.

And he loved us.

He loved his sister, Meg. Three years and two months separate Nate and Meg. Sibling rivalry was the order of the day. And so was love. They fought and hugged. They disagreed and made up. There was no accident that Nate and Meg are brother and sister. Without Nate, Meg would not be the incredible woman of sensitivity and caring that she is. Without Meg, Nate would never have known sharing and leadership.

He loved his brother, Colin. Almost eleven years separate Nate and Colin. And those early years of the two of them together were so precious. Nate taught Colin to walk, to run, to laugh, and to lead. When Colin could only say his own name as "Lue-Lue," Nate eventually put a brotherly end to that. "Dude, Lue-Lue is a girl's name. From now on you *will* be called "'Lue'"—and Lue it was, to Nate and to many of us.

He loved his mom, Susan. His years of being homeschooled brought about a special bond between mother and son, teacher and student. Nate had reading difficulties, and he had the right teacher to help him through that. Susan taught Nate about life and love and commitment.

As he left homeschooling in fourth grade, his teachers at Boise's Cole Christian School, Mrs. Janet Schultz and Mrs. Joan Oster, took the baton and led him on. Susan remained his teacher in life, and it was an honor for me to watch him with her. I saw that relationship blossom into adulthood. How blessed I was to be a participant, but also to just be an observer, at times.

Susan's last visit, in person, with Nate was actually on his twenty-seventh birthday, this past July. How fitting for that to have occurred. It would be our final birthday celebration with our son Nate. Susan and he kissed and said good-bye to each other, unknowingly for the last time.

He loved his fiancée, Ginny. And she was with him until the end. Ginny, thank you for the three-plus years of love, care, and support you gave to Nate. He was never abandoned after prison, because he had you, and he had his precious dogs, Satchel and Clarice. Your "family" with him lives on through Meg's dog, Stella. May your future be bright because of your brilliant memories of Nate.

He loved his best friend, Mark Smit, and awaits him in Heaven. Nate was loyal to his other friends—those men who carry him today in his casket. He was loyal to all his other friends—both to those who helped and to those who hurt him.

Nate's adult years had pain but were not defined by pain. Few sofas were sent ahead during these years. Nate's disease of substance abuse held him in its grip, but he was not an addict. He was a believer in Jesus Christ who desperately struggled with drug abuse. He wanted a way out but found no clear open doors.

That truth and subsequent pain encouraged us four years ago to birth a simple little Bible study in Ada County Jail that has led thousands to Christ.

Which in turn led Susan and me to invite Mac and Dianne Mayer to help us help others who, like Nate, want to overcome their struggle with substance abuse but need help.

We do it through faith and hope in Jesus. Addiction affects the whole community. Our efforts brought about staffed, safe, and sober homes. We're sending a sofa on ahead, aren't we, Nate?

You are already sitting on it, aren't you, Son?

Nate lives. In Heaven, he is alive, sitting on his sofa, waiting for us—smiling that teasing smile.

And in the lives of men and women overcoming addiction, Nate Mansfield rejoices in eternity.

I end with this.

When Nate was a year old, I began journaling after hearing a television interview with the actor Lloyd Bridges. The well-respected television and motion picture professional spoke passionately about how he recorded by pen and paper the events of his children's lives. He began the journaling when they were babies with the express desire that when he and his wife had raised them to adulthood and each was about to be married, he would give bound volumes of his entries to each of his adult sons' or daughter's new spouse. He wanted each new member to his family to truly know whom they were marrying. That was good enough for me, so I began journaling.

I wrote about our life as a family and about each child. Every year, I purchased a crisp new blank journal book and every December, I placed it, worn and ragged, into a place of safe-keeping.

I have done so for twenty-nine years. When my daughter was married in 2003, she received two bound volumes of journal entries about her life, from birth to just a little before the wedding. Nate was to receive the same type of gift at his wedding.

I'd like to read the very first journal entry that had Nate's name in it, and I'd like to close with a journal entry from a little over a week ago.

*July 28, 1981*

*In your goals and desires, keep paramount the question: Is what I am doing pleasing to God. Don't worry about Mom and Dad, we're pleased that God even loaned you to us.*

*March 11, 2009*

*My precious son, Nate, died today at around noon. He died in his sleep and my heart almost stopped. I never anticipated journaling the death of any child. Today is that day. For twenty-six years, I've written of Nate's life, his honors, his failures and his comebacks. Today, on this date, Nate goes from being referred to as "is" to "was." His life ended today on this side of the veil. On the other side he now resides. Forever. I began journaling about him and his life, Meg and her life, Colin and his life. I wrote and wrote about all of life. I was twenty-seven years old when I started. Nate is twenty-seven years old as I finish writing about his life today.*

*Nathan Dennis Mansfield was a good, hard, fair-focused, vocal, loving man. He was passionate and loved to give his opinion. His love language was quality time, and he was a High I on the DISC test. Disorganized, messy, movie loving, and generous, Nate loved all and feared none. He taught me to love coaching, Twix candy bars, and laughter. I introduced him to Dr Pepper, all sports, Jim Rome, conservative politics, and most importantly to Jesus Christ. He rests with the Creator of the Universe and loves his Ginger, his dogs Satchel and Clarice, his folks, his Meg and his Colin.*

# Death's Diamonds

Time wasn't on his side. Neither were his genes. He was a fourteen-year-old juvenile delinquent with parents who died early. He had inherited a set of lungs full of liquid from his father's side of the family that seemed to be working nightly to bring him into the darkness of death. Donello Simone was sick—and very tired.

Donny was angry. Each night he felt sure that this was it, the last one, and it seemed that each night made his condition worse. But come the next morning, he would awake with the same smug statement: "I'm still here. You can't touch me."

The house was hardly a home. Weather-beaten, unkempt, and unpainted, it was a place to sleep during the night and a neighborhood to avoid in the daytime. His parents had been dead since he turned ten and this lean-to shack was the best his Italian grandmother had to offer an orphan.

That and her love—a love he returned. He was anxious; he wanted to move on. Though the past four years showed him the love of his grandmom, he simply wanted to move on.

Then his day came. But oddly, he wasn't the one to leave.

Late in the midafternoon of a cold February day, his grandmother slumped in her chair, dropped her book, and silently slipped into another world.

Donny was left in this world, a complete orphan with no family, no next of kin, and only a lousy piece of real estate owned by the dead woman now sitting across from him.

Two weeks had elapsed. Jasper Shantel was an evil man; worse than that, he was an evil attorney. He was the kind of fat, sloppy, and southern variety who may have been used later as the example for John Candy to play in the horribly unhistorical film *JFK*. He was fat, sweaty, and careless.

Shantel knew the corner lot was valuable. Elise Simone was eighty-six years and dead; she was old, but she had not been a fool when she was alive. When death took her by surprise, she was, in a funny way, prepared. She'd long ago put the corner lot real estate in her grandson's name.

"Fuggetabout the IRS, fuggetabout my other kids, who haven't seen me in years," she had said to Donny just a short time before she died. She always had an odd, awkward smile—as though she was hiding something. "Donny's the only one who's ever cared for me. He's the only one who gets my help—either here while I am alive or there when that fat Mississippi lawyer reads the will."

And Jasper Shantel *did* read it. Out loud to an audience of Elise's kids, siblings, and attorneys. You see, Elise's land sat on the most desired corner in Manhattan. The year was 1962 and Donny Simone was now land rich.

Soon he'd be cash rich and not worried about education. "School? I'm ready to register for the school of life, now—and pay cash," he said with a smile.

Nineteen seventy-four brought twenty-six-year-old Donello (as he now preferred to be called) a year unlike any of the past dozen. He was Italian, wealthy, and without any accountability.

He was flanked by nearby shadowy men with binoculars who protected him, always scanning the horizon.

Then the wealth of youth met the experience of men twice his age and not even near his level of financial wealth. They were con men who "helped" others by separating them from their cash. They wanted to help Donello Simone.

Names aren't important except one: Weinstein.

Weinstein was the name of the neighborhood, or was it a family? Donello never quite knew. It was an area of con men, crank addicts, whores, and thieves.

They came into his office. Donello's security guards were absent. "May I help you?" he asked.

Donello's body jerked three times in response to his own question, as the triple shotgun blast shook the dust from ceiling fans on floors far below. Then the silent overcoated men left, and as they shut the door, one turned back with an evil red glare in his eye and smiled. Donello lay dying; the red eyes, his last vision of the living, those eyes were worse than death. Darkness consumed Donny as he heard an unfamiliar voice, then he was gone and all that was left was the smoke and shot, blood and death everywhere.

He left it all behind as the sound became more recognizable; now he looked for eternal answers.

Donny was being transferred in his spirit. A white, bright light of diamonds and the crystal-clear sounds of voices met his senses; someone was calling his name.

No, that wasn't right, he wasn't being called, he was being announced. He couldn't help but know that there was life after death—he was there. He was in Heaven and he was about to be judged.

*To be continued . . .*

*—By Nate and Dennis Mansfield*
*along with Caleb Roe and Colin Mansfield © 2009 and 2012*

# Acknowledgments

My deepest thanks are extended to four groups of people.

Those who allowed this work to be placed in your hands:

• Paul and Virginia Friesen, for allowing me to write this book while at Campus by the Sea and for loving the Mansfields, decade after decade.

• My friends at Simon and Schuster (Howard)—Philis Boulting-house, who believed in this book idea out of her own pain and did a fantastic job on editing and amending my skills. Thank you. Amanda Demastus, Amy Ryan, and the staff members whom I have not yet met but were impacted by this story enough to agree in its publishing. You all changed my life.

• Brandon McKey—who, while sitting with me at Campus by the Sea, helped me end each chapter well. He and his Susan loved Nate as though he was theirs. Thank you.

• My friend and agent, Chris Ferrebee, of Chris Ferrebee and Associates, who suggested that I write this book. Chris, you gambled on a "Who's he?" Thank you.

- Larry Kelley, my friend and business partner with 8:4 Pictures. You and Nate never met, but your spirits for movies were identical.

Those who loved Susan and me as we entered the monarchy of the Master:

- My sisters Janet, for the long car ride in the summer of '77, and Joyce, for the long letter in '79. Both moved me into the kingdom of Christ.

- Tom and Pat Harris, who led us to Christ; Cass Schreib, our first pastor; and all those in our first smoky AA Bible study.

- John and Leah VanderWende, who prayed us into the kingdom.

- Woody Wood, who loved me then and loves me now as his brother (and his bride, Danica, who came into our lives and into our hearts.)

- Pam and Henri Raynaud, for using photography to capture and record years of love, while laughing, wrestling, and loving our combined four (then five!) kids.

- Christa Marvin, Susan's prayer partner for decades. Thank you for your prayers about Nate, Meg, and Colin.

- Peter and Barb Gozdeck, for asking us the question, "Do you want to?" and Peter, for mentoring me all these years.

Those significant adults who in Nate's life loved him unconditionally:

- Paul, Diane, Taryn, and Mark Smit—Nate's second family. Thank you for all the sweet holiday memories together. Mark, thanks for your brotherly love of Nate.

• Larry and Vonda Rampenthal, Nate's maternal grandparents.

• My father, Bill Mansfield, who passed into eternity during the final editing of this book and was met at the gates of Heaven by Nate.

• My mother, Virginia Maguire Mansfield, who welcomed Nate into Heaven as well.

• Susan's mother, Wanda Wilcox McKay, whom Nate welcomed into Heaven just seven short weeks later.

• *My siblings:* Kathy, Gary, Janet, JoAnne, Joyce, Ken, Diane, and Cheri. *Susan's siblings:* Debby, Larry, JoAn, and Cathy.

• Terry and Francie Bush, who loved "Nater" as if he were their own son—and who introduced us all to Campus by the Sea.

• John and Ellen Price and their son, Derek, who accepted and loved Nate for who he was.

• Kevin and Alison Hearon, for loving Nate from start to finish. He would have been a great chiropractor!

• Our extended family, all of whom hold warm memories of Nathan, Nater Potato, and Nate.

• Michael Boerner, Bill Proctor, and Russ Fulcher, for being great examples of men to Nate. He loved you three so much.

• Steve Switzer, Nate's godfather, friend, and foil—he loved you so much.

• Ginny, Nate's love—thank you for caring for Nate, for loving him, and for wanting to marry him. He loved you so.

*Acknowledgments*

Lastly, my family:

- My daughter, Meg, and son-in-law, Caleb—for loving Nate at all times. You are an example to me of selfless love. Nate knew it, Satchel knew it, I know it. Meg, Nate loved you so much.

- My son Colin—for loving Nate from your little-boy years into adolescence. You were always his Lue, and he was always proud of you. He still is. Col, Nate loved you so much.

- My bride, Susan, who helped me clearly remember Nate's life, through tears and smiles, from his first breath to the very day of his death. This may be my story, but your signature is on every page. Thank you for giving Nater to me.

- Nate—thank you for showing me that the heart of God is not always neat and tidy, that God's love is unconditional, and that Jesus paid it *all*; gifts given aren't earned, and if we'll be honest with ourselves, we're all broken—in need of Christ's healing hand for eternity. I look forward to sitting on your sofa with you. —Daddio.

Printed in the United States
By Bookmasters